ALIGNED FOR PURPOSE

Whole by Design: The Five Pillars of a God-Centered Life

Emerald M Burke

Copyright © [2026] [**Emerald M Burke**].

All rights reserved.

No part of this publication may be reproduced, distributed, or transmitted in any form or by any means, including photocopying, recording, or other electronic or mechanical methods, without the prior written permission of the author or publisher, except in the case of brief quotations embodied in critical reviews and certain other noncommercial uses permitted by copyright law.

Table of Contents

Introduction — Aligned for Purpose 1

Chapter 1 — Spiritual Foundation: Living Rooted, Not Rushed 5

Chapter 2 — Mental Renewal: Reclaiming the Way You Think 11

Chapter 3 — Emotional Wholeness: Healing What Life Has Broken . 18

Chapter 4 — Physical Stewardship: Honoring the Body God Gave You 25

Chapter 5 — Financial Responsibility: Stewardship Without Fear or Shame 31

Chapter 6 — Integration: Living an Aligned Life Without Fragmentation 40

Chapter 7 — Mental Renewal: Understanding the Battlefield of the Mind 47

Chapter 8 — Emotional Resilience: Remaining Steady When Life Is Unstable 54

Chapter 9 — Emotional Healing in Relationships: Restoring Trust Without Losing Yourself 61

Chapter 10 — Emotional Freedom: Releasing the Past Without Carrying It Forward 69

Chapter 11 — Physical Discipline: Building Strength That Sustains Purpose 77

Chapter 12 — Physical Rest and Recovery: Sustaining Purpose Without Burnout 84

Chapter 13 — Mental Clarity and Focus: Quieting the Noise That Dilutes Purpose 92

Chapter 14 — Decision-Making With Wisdom: Choosing Alignment Over Impulse 99

Chapter 15 — Purpose in the Waiting: Faithfulness When Progress Feels Slow 107

Chapter 16 — When Faith Becomes a Way of Life: Living Aligned Every Day 114

Chapter 16 — When Faith Becomes a Way of Life: Living Aligned Every Day 121

Chapter 17 — Walking in Obedience: Choosing God's Way When It Costs You 128

Chapter 18 — Endurance and Perseverance: Staying Faithful When the Journey Is Long 136

Chapter 19 — Financial Peace and Provision: Living Free From the Grip of Fear 143

Chapter 20 — Generational Impact: Living So Others Are Changed Because You Lived 151

Chapter 21 — Leadership Through Service: Influence Rooted in Humility and Responsibility 159

Chapter 22 — Accountability and Integrity: Living the Same in Private as in Public 167

Chapter 23 — Community and Connection: Thriving Through God-Centered Relationships 175

Chapter 24 — Healing and Restoration: Allowing God to Repair What Life Has Wounded 183

Chapter 25 — Identity and Worth: Living From Who God Says You Are 191

Chapter 26 — Resilience Through Change: Remaining Aligned When Life Shifts 199

Chapter 27 — Living With Discernment in a Confused World 207

Chapter 28 — Discipline That Sustains Freedom 214

Chapter 29 — Purpose Beyond Circumstances 222

Chapter 30 — Walking in Daily Alignment: Living the Five Pillars as One Life 230

Chapter 31 — When All Five Pillars Work Together: The Life God Designed to Function as One 239

Chapter 32 — The Life That Reflects God's Design: Real-World Traits and Daily Application 248

Final Conclusion — Choosing Alignment as a Way of Life 257

Introduction

Aligned for Purpose

Life becomes exhausting when it is lived out of alignment.

Many people love God, work hard, and care deeply about others, yet still feel unsettled — as if something is always off. Faith exists, but peace feels fragile. Prayer happens, but clarity is inconsistent. There is movement, effort, and sacrifice, yet progress feels scattered. This sense of imbalance is not accidental. It is the result of living without alignment to God's full design.

Aligned for Purpose was written to restore that alignment.

God never intended human life to be lived in fragments. From the beginning, His design was whole — spirit, mind, heart, body, and resources working together in harmony. When these areas are disconnected, life becomes reactive instead of intentional. Burnout replaces peace. Confusion replaces direction. Survival replaces purpose.

This book is rooted in one foundational truth: **alignment precedes effectiveness**. When life is aligned with God's design, purpose becomes clearer, decisions become steadier, and growth becomes sustainable.

This is not a book about perfection. It is a book about **order**.

Understanding Alignment

Alignment means living in agreement with how something was created to function. When a structure is misaligned, it may still stand for a time, but stress builds beneath the surface. Cracks appear. Repairs become constant. Eventually, something gives way.

The same is true in life.

Many people are spiritually committed but mentally overwhelmed. Others are emotionally generous but physically depleted. Some are financially productive but spiritually disconnected. These imbalances do not mean failure — they mean something is out of order.

God's response is not condemnation.
It is invitation.

Alignment does not require rebuilding your life from scratch. It requires returning to God's design and allowing Him to reorder what has drifted.

The Purpose Behind This Book

Aligned for Purpose exists to bring clarity to areas of life that are often addressed separately but lived together. Faith is not meant to be practiced only in church. It is meant to guide thinking, emotions, habits, health, and stewardship every day.

This book provides a **biblical framework for everyday living**, grounded in Scripture and shaped by real life. It speaks to people navigating responsibility, stress, leadership, caregiving, rebuilding seasons, delayed dreams, and silent struggles.

Rather than offering quick fixes, this book focuses on foundation. Rather than pushing performance, it teaches alignment. Purpose is not found by doing more — it is revealed by living in agreement with God.

The Five Pillars of an Aligned Life

This book is structured around five essential pillars that reflect God's original design for wholeness:

Spiritual Foundation

Living rooted in God rather than driven by pressure, fear, or urgency. This pillar addresses relationship with God, trust, obedience, discernment, and spiritual stability in real-life situations.

Mental Renewal

Restoring clarity to the mind and breaking cycles of fear, anxiety, overthinking, and mental fatigue. This pillar explores how thoughts shape decisions, faith, and behavior.

Emotional Wholeness

Healing what life has damaged. This pillar addresses emotional wounds, forgiveness, boundaries, maturity, and learning how to feel without being controlled by emotions.

Physical Stewardship

Honoring the body as a gift rather than an afterthought. This pillar explores discipline, rest, balance, and the connection between physical health and spiritual effectiveness.

Financial Responsibility

Managing resources with wisdom, peace, and purpose. This pillar addresses stewardship, provision, generosity, discipline, and freedom from financial stress.

Each pillar contains **six full chapters**, allowing for depth, reflection, and real-life application without rushing the process.

How to Read and Apply This Book

This book is meant to be lived with, not rushed through.

Readers may choose to read from beginning to end, focus on one pillar at a time, or return to chapters as seasons change. Growth does not happen on a schedule. Alignment happens through understanding, reflection, and daily choices.

Each chapter is written to:

- explain the principle clearly
- connect Scripture to everyday life
- address real struggles honestly
- encourage sustainable change

Scripture is woven naturally throughout the content and referenced at the end of each chapter for deeper study, allowing the reading experience to remain smooth and grounded in God's Word.

Who This Book Is For

This book is for people who love God but feel stretched thin.
For those who are faithful yet tired.

For those rebuilding after loss, trauma, delay, or disappointment.
For anyone who senses they were made for more but feels out of alignment.

You do not need to do more.

You need to live **aligned for purpose**.

Wholeness was never accidental.

It was always the design.

Chapter 1

Spiritual Foundation: Living Rooted, Not Rushed

A spiritually grounded life reshapes how a person understands pressure. Pressure no longer feels like an emergency that must be escaped but a signal that alignment is required. When life presses in, a rooted believer does not immediately ask, *"How do I fix this?"* Instead, they ask, *"What is God forming in me here?"* That shift changes everything. Pressure no longer produces panic; it produces perspective.

Pressure reveals foundation. It exposes whether faith is reactive or rooted, whether trust is shallow or deep. Many people discover the fragility of their spiritual foundation only when life becomes heavy. Loss, financial strain, betrayal, illness, responsibility, or transition often expose how much faith has been built on comfort rather than conviction. This exposure is painful, but it is also merciful. God does not reveal weakness to shame — He reveals it to strengthen.

Spiritual foundation is built when faith is practiced consistently in ordinary moments, not only in crisis. It is formed quietly through daily decisions to trust God when outcomes are uncertain, to obey Him when obedience feels inconvenient, and to remain faithful when progress feels slow. These moments rarely feel spiritual while they are happening, yet they are the very moments where roots grow deepest.

When Faith Becomes Conditional

One of the most common threats to spiritual grounding is conditional faith. Conditional faith trusts God as long as life unfolds in expected ways. It believes as long as prayers are answered quickly. It rests as long as circumstances remain manageable. When life deviates from expectation, conditional faith begins to weaken.

Scripture does not define faith as agreement with outcomes. It defines faith as confidence in God's character. A rooted spiritual life does not depend on visible progress to remain steady. It depends on the belief that God is present, faithful, and at work even when progress is unseen.

Many believers struggle here. They believe God is good, but wrestle with trusting Him when obedience requires waiting, loss, or sacrifice. This struggle does not disqualify faith; it reveals where faith needs to deepen. God does not ask people to ignore uncertainty. He invites them to bring uncertainty to Him instead of allowing it to control their decisions.

When faith becomes conditional, peace becomes fragile. When trust is rooted in outcomes, disappointment becomes destabilizing. A strong spiritual foundation shifts trust away from circumstances and anchors it in God's consistency.

Obedience Without Full Clarity

One of the most difficult aspects of spiritual alignment is obedience without full understanding. Modern life teaches people to gather information, evaluate risk, and secure certainty before acting. Biblical faith often requires the opposite. Scripture repeatedly shows God calling people to move before outcomes are clear, to trust before details are revealed, and to obey before reassurance arrives.

This does not make faith reckless. It makes faith relational.

A rooted believer learns to act on conviction rather than comfort. They understand that clarity often comes *after* obedience, not before. Many delays in spiritual growth occur not because God is silent, but because people are waiting for certainty God never promised. Faith matures when obedience is chosen even when the full picture remains unseen.

This kind of obedience builds spiritual confidence. Each act of trust strengthens the ability to trust again. Over time, obedience without full clarity becomes less frightening and more familiar, because experience confirms God's faithfulness.

Discernment Versus Urgency

Spiritual foundation sharpens discernment. Discernment is the ability to distinguish God's voice from fear, pressure, emotion, or personal desire. Without discernment, urgency masquerades as calling and emotion replaces instruction. Over time, this creates exhaustion and confusion.

God's guidance carries peace, even when it calls for courage. Panic and pressure are rarely indicators of divine direction. A rooted spiritual life learns to pause before responding, to pray before committing, and to wait when direction is unclear. This does not slow purpose — it protects it.

Many people confuse movement with progress. They rush decisions because they fear missing opportunities or disappointing others. Spiritual grounding teaches that what is truly meant for you will not require anxiety to obtain. Discernment grows through time spent with God, familiarity with His Word, and the discipline of waiting when answers are delayed.

The Discipline of Waiting

Waiting is one of the most misunderstood spiritual disciplines. It is often viewed as passive, unproductive, or frustrating. Scripture presents waiting as active trust — the decision to remain faithful without forcing outcomes.

Waiting exposes internal restlessness. It reveals how much identity has become attached to productivity, achievement, or control. When waiting feels unbearable, it often indicates that trust is still developing. God uses waiting to realign motives, purify intentions, and deepen dependence.

A rooted spiritual life understands that waiting does not delay purpose. It prepares a person to carry it. Strength developed through waiting sustains purpose when movement resumes.

Identity Before Assignment

Another cornerstone of spiritual foundation is identity. Many believers unknowingly build their identity on what they do for God rather than who they are with Him. This creates performance-based faith — faith that feels valuable only when productive, visible, or affirmed.

Performance-based faith is exhausting. It turns rest into guilt and boundaries into selfishness. Scripture teaches a different identity — one rooted in relationship rather than results. God's people are loved, called, and valued before they act. Obedience flows from identity; it does not create it.

A spiritually grounded person serves from fullness rather than striving. Their worth is not threatened by rest, and their faith is not shaken by seasons of stillness. This understanding frees obedience from pressure and restores joy to service.

Stability in Seasons of Change

Spiritual foundation becomes especially critical during seasons of transition. Change disrupts routine, challenges certainty, and exposes insecurity. Without grounding, transitions produce anxiety and impulsive decisions. With grounding, transitions become seasons of refinement.

Scripture shows God leading His people through transition repeatedly — from wilderness to promise, from obscurity to calling, from loss to restoration. Stability in these seasons never came from circumstances; it came from trust. A rooted believer anchors themselves in God's consistency rather than situational security.

Transitions test foundation, but they also strengthen it. When navigated with trust, they deepen alignment and sharpen purpose.

Living Rooted Daily

Spiritual alignment is not achieved once. It is practiced daily. It is choosing prayer over panic, obedience over impulse, trust over control. These choices are rarely dramatic, yet they shape everything.

A rooted spiritual life does not make a person perfect. It makes them stable. Stability allows faith to endure pressure, purpose to unfold without strain, and peace to remain even when life is uncertain.

Purpose flows from alignment, not effort. When life is spiritually rooted, direction becomes clearer, endurance becomes possible, and growth becomes sustainable. This foundation supports every other area of life — mental clarity, emotional healing, physical discipline, and financial stewardship.

To live **Aligned for Purpose**, spiritual foundation must come first. Everything else builds upon it.

Scriptures Referenced in This Chapter

- Psalm 1:1–3
- Proverbs 3:5–6
- Matthew 6:33
- Isaiah 40:31
- Luke 5:16
- John 15:4–7
- Hebrews 11:1–6
- James 1:2–4

Chapter 2

Mental Renewal: Reclaiming the Way You Think

The mind is one of the most powerful and misunderstood battlegrounds in life.

Many people love God sincerely yet live mentally exhausted, overwhelmed, and trapped in cycles of negative thinking. Faith is present, but peace feels inconsistent. Prayer happens, yet anxiety lingers. Hope exists, but clarity feels distant. This disconnect often causes believers to question themselves, wondering why spiritual devotion has not translated into mental rest.

The issue is rarely a lack of faith.

More often, it is a lack of **mental alignment**.

God designed the mind to be renewed, not tormented. Yet without intentional renewal, the mind defaults to survival patterns shaped by experience, trauma, stress, and repetition. Thoughts left unchecked begin to shape beliefs. Beliefs shape decisions. Decisions shape life.

Mental renewal is not optional for a purposeful life. It is foundational.

The Mind as a Gatekeeper

The mind functions as a gatekeeper. What is allowed to dwell there eventually influences emotions, behaviors, and spiritual perception.

Scripture consistently emphasizes the importance of guarding the mind because God understands its power. A mind left unmanaged becomes a breeding ground for fear, doubt, and distortion.

Many people assume their thoughts are neutral or harmless, but thoughts are rarely passive. Repeated thoughts become internal narratives, and internal narratives eventually become identity statements. What a person repeatedly tells themselves will begin to feel true, even when it is not.

This is why mental renewal is essential to living aligned for purpose. A misaligned mind can sabotage even the strongest calling.

How Mental Patterns Are Formed

Mental patterns do not form overnight. They develop slowly through repetition and reinforcement. Experiences, words spoken over us, disappointments, failures, and trauma all contribute to how the mind learns to interpret the world.

For some, mental patterns are shaped by scarcity.
For others, by rejection.
For many, by survival.

When someone has lived in instability, the mind often learns to expect loss. When someone has experienced betrayal, the mind learns to anticipate harm. When someone has endured repeated disappointment, the mind begins to protect itself through pessimism.

These patterns are not signs of weakness. They are signs of adaptation. However, what once protected the mind can later imprison it.

God's design for the mind is not constant defense — it is renewal.

The Difference Between Thoughts and Truth

One of the most freeing realizations in mental renewal is understanding that thoughts are not facts.

Thoughts are impressions, reactions, memories, and interpretations. They are influenced by mood, fatigue, environment, and past experience. Yet many people treat every thought as truth simply because it appears in their mind.

This is where mental bondage begins.

A renewed mind learns to pause and evaluate thoughts rather than immediately agreeing with them. It learns to ask, *"Is this thought aligned with truth, or is it shaped by fear, habit, or past pain?"*

Scripture teaches that truth brings freedom, not confusion. When thoughts consistently produce fear, shame, or hopelessness, they deserve examination. God does not speak through condemnation or chaos. His guidance brings clarity, conviction, and peace — even when it challenges.

Mental renewal requires learning how to separate truth from familiarity. Lies often feel familiar because they have been repeated for years.

Fear, Anxiety, and Overthinking

Fear is one of the most dominant forces shaping the modern mind. Fear of failure, fear of lack, fear of rejection, fear of loss — all contribute to chronic overthinking and mental exhaustion. Anxiety is often not about the present moment, but about anticipated outcomes that may never occur.

A mind consumed by fear struggles to trust God fully. Not because trust is absent, but because fear speaks louder. Mental renewal quiets fear by reestablishing perspective.

Scripture repeatedly addresses fear because it understands how easily fear distorts perception. Fear magnifies problems and minimizes God. Renewal reverses that pattern. It does not deny challenges; it restores proportion.

Overthinking is often a form of self-protection. The mind attempts to prevent harm by anticipating every possible outcome. Unfortunately, this only creates fatigue and indecision. A renewed mind learns when to think and when to release.

God did not design the mind to carry infinite possibilities. He designed it to walk daily in trust.

Renewal Requires Intentional Replacement

Mental renewal is not achieved by simply trying to "think positive." It requires intentional replacement. Old patterns must be confronted and replaced with truth repeatedly until new patterns form.

Scripture emphasizes transformation through renewal, not suppression. Suppressing thoughts does not remove them; it often strengthens them. Renewal requires acknowledgment, evaluation, and replacement.

This process takes time. The mind does not change overnight because it was not shaped overnight. Renewal is gradual, layered, and deeply personal.

Each time a fearful thought is replaced with truth, renewal strengthens. Each time a lie is challenged, mental freedom increases. Over time, the mind becomes a place of clarity rather than chaos.

Rest and Mental Alignment

Rest is a critical component of mental renewal. Many mental struggles are intensified by exhaustion. A tired mind is more vulnerable to fear, irritability, and hopelessness. God designed rest as a safeguard, not a reward.

Scripture consistently connects rest with trust. Rest requires surrender — the belief that life will not fall apart if productivity pauses. This belief is difficult for those whose identity has been shaped by survival or performance.

A renewed mind learns to rest without guilt. It understands that clarity often emerges in stillness. Many answers are not discovered through effort, but through rest.

Mental alignment improves dramatically when rest is honored consistently.

Discipline Without Harshness

Mental discipline is often misunderstood as harsh self-control. Biblical discipline is different. It is gentle, consistent guidance that leads the mind back to alignment when it wanders.

A renewed mind learns to redirect rather than punish itself. It does not shame itself for intrusive thoughts or emotional reactions. Instead, it recognizes them as signals and responds with wisdom.

Self-condemnation weakens renewal. Grace strengthens it.

God does not demand perfection of thought. He invites transformation through relationship and patience.

The Role of Scripture in Mental Renewal

Scripture functions as an anchor for the mind. It provides a standard of truth that does not shift with emotion or circumstance. When Scripture is internalized, it becomes a filter through which thoughts are evaluated.

Mental renewal deepens when Scripture moves from being referenced to being believed. This happens gradually, as truth is applied repeatedly in real-life situations.

Scripture does not silence the mind; it stabilizes it.

Mental Renewal in Daily Life

Mental renewal is practiced in ordinary moments — during decisions, conversations, disappointments, and delays. It is choosing to pause instead of spiraling, to pray instead of panic, to trust instead of assume the worst.

A renewed mind does not eliminate struggle. It transforms response.

When the mind is aligned:

- anxiety loses its grip
- decisions become clearer
- faith feels steadier
- peace becomes accessible

Mental renewal restores authority over thoughts rather than allowing thoughts to dominate life.

Alignment Produces Clarity

Purpose requires clarity. Clarity requires renewal.

A misaligned mind can distort calling, sabotage relationships, and exhaust the soul. A renewed mind supports spiritual foundation, emotional healing, physical discipline, and financial wisdom.

God's desire is not mental survival.
It is mental freedom.

To live **Aligned for Purpose**, the mind must be renewed intentionally, patiently, and consistently. This renewal creates space for peace, endurance, and wisdom to grow.

Scriptures Referenced in This Chapter

- Romans 12:2
- 2 Timothy 1:7
- Philippians 4:6–8
- Isaiah 26:3
- Proverbs 4:23
- 2 Corinthians 10:3–5
- Psalm 94:19

Chapter 3

Emotional Wholeness: Healing What Life Has Broken

Emotional health shapes how a person experiences life far more than most people realize. It influences how relationships form, how conflict is handled, how trust develops, and how faith is expressed under pressure. Many people appear functional on the outside while carrying deep emotional fractures on the inside. They work, serve, pray, and care for others, yet privately struggle with anger, fear, numbness, or exhaustion they cannot explain.

God never designed people to live emotionally fractured.

Emotional wholeness is not the absence of pain. It is the ability to process pain without allowing it to control identity, decisions, or purpose. When emotional wounds are ignored, they do not disappear — they surface later in unhealthy ways. When they are acknowledged and healed, life begins to feel lighter, clearer, and more stable.

Emotional healing is not optional for an aligned life. It is essential.

How Emotional Wounds Are Formed

Emotional wounds are rarely caused by a single moment. More often, they develop through repeated experiences — abandonment, rejection, neglect, betrayal, disappointment, or being forced to grow up too soon. Over time, these experiences teach the heart how to protect itself.

Some people learn to harden emotionally.
Others learn to overattach.
Some learn to suppress feelings.
Others become overwhelmed by them.

These responses are not signs of weakness. They are survival strategies. However, what once protected the heart can later imprison it.

God's design for emotional life was never survival — it was connection.

When emotional wounds go unaddressed, they quietly shape behavior. Trust becomes difficult. Vulnerability feels dangerous. Relationships feel draining. Faith becomes inconsistent. Many people do not realize they are living from wounded places because those wounds have become familiar.

Healing begins with awareness.

Permission to Feel Without Shame

One of the greatest barriers to emotional wholeness is shame around emotions. Many people were taught, directly or indirectly, that expressing emotion is a sign of weakness. Others learned that emotions are inconvenient or unacceptable. As a result, feelings were buried rather than processed.

Scripture presents a very different picture.

Throughout Scripture, people express grief, fear, anger, confusion, joy, and sorrow openly before God. They cry out. They question. They lament. God does not rebuke them for feeling — He meets them in it.

Emotional honesty is not spiritual failure.
It is spiritual maturity.

Healing requires permission to feel without judgment. When emotions are suppressed, they intensify. When they are acknowledged, they begin to lose their control. God invites honesty because He understands that healing cannot occur where truth is denied.

The Connection Between Belief and Emotion

Emotional wounds often attach themselves to beliefs formed during vulnerable moments. These beliefs may never be spoken aloud, yet they quietly influence life for years.

Beliefs such as:

- "I am not enough."
- "People always leave."
- "I have to earn love."
- "I can't trust anyone."
- "God didn't protect me."

These beliefs shape expectations, reactions, and decisions. They influence how people interpret events and how they respond emotionally. Even when faith is present, unhealed beliefs can distort perception.

Emotional wholeness requires identifying and replacing beliefs that no longer align with truth. This process takes time and patience. God does not rush healing because trust is rebuilt gradually.

Truth does not invalidate pain — it redeems it.

Forgiveness as Emotional Release

Forgiveness is one of the most misunderstood aspects of emotional healing. Many people resist forgiveness because they equate it with excusing harm or minimizing pain. Scripture presents forgiveness differently.

Forgiveness is not approval.
It is not forgetting.
It is not reconciliation without wisdom.

Forgiveness is the release of the right to remain emotionally bound to an offense.

Unforgiveness keeps pain active. It replays wounds repeatedly and ties emotional energy to the past. Forgiveness interrupts that cycle. It does not deny what happened; it releases its control.

God commands forgiveness not to burden people, but to free them. Emotional wholeness cannot coexist with ongoing resentment. Forgiveness creates space for peace to grow.

This process is often gradual. Forgiveness may need to be chosen repeatedly before emotional relief fully settles. God honors that process.

Boundaries and Emotional Safety

Boundaries are a critical component of emotional health. Many emotionally wounded people struggle with boundaries because they confuse love with access. Scripture teaches that wisdom includes discernment — knowing when to engage and when to step back.

Jesus loved deeply, yet He withdrew often. He did not explain Himself to everyone. He did not remain in harmful environments. He honored limits without guilt.

Boundaries protect emotional safety. They prevent repeated harm and create space for healing. Without boundaries, emotional wounds are continually reopened.

Setting boundaries is not rejection.
It is stewardship of the heart.

A healed emotional life understands that saying no can be an act of obedience. Boundaries allow relationships to exist in healthier forms rather than being driven by fear or obligation.

Emotional Maturity Versus Emotional Suppression

Emotional maturity is not the absence of emotion. It is the ability to experience emotion without being ruled by it. Suppressing emotions does not create maturity — it creates delayed reactions.

When emotions are ignored, they surface later as anger, anxiety, depression, or detachment. Emotional maturity learns how to feel fully while responding wisely.

God designed emotions as indicators, not dictators. They signal what is happening internally, but they are not meant to control decisions. A mature emotional life listens to emotions without surrendering authority to them.

This balance develops through practice. It requires patience, reflection, and grace. Emotional growth does not happen overnight because trust takes time to rebuild.

Healing Takes Time and Layers

One of the most important truths about emotional healing is that it happens in layers. God often heals gradually, addressing wounds as trust deepens. Immediate healing is possible, but lasting healing is often progressive.

Many people become discouraged when healing feels slow. They assume something is wrong. Scripture shows that growth often occurs through process. God values depth over speed.

Each layer of healing strengthens emotional resilience. Over time, reactions soften, peace becomes steadier, and relationships become healthier. Emotional wholeness does not erase memory — it redeems meaning.

Emotional Health and Faith

Unhealed emotional wounds can distort faith. They can cause people to project past pain onto God, struggle with trust, or withdraw spiritually. Healing restores clarity.

When emotional health improves:

- prayer becomes more honest
- trust becomes possible again
- faith becomes steadier
- peace becomes accessible

God desires wholeness in every area because each area affects the others. Emotional healing strengthens spiritual foundation and supports mental renewal.

Living Emotionally Whole

Living emotionally whole does not mean life becomes painless. It means pain no longer defines identity. It means emotions are processed rather than suppressed. It means forgiveness replaces bitterness and boundaries replace fear.

An emotionally whole life creates space for joy, connection, and peace. It allows people to love without losing themselves and to trust without abandoning wisdom.

God does not want His people emotionally surviving.
He wants them emotionally free.

To live **Aligned for Purpose**, emotional healing must be embraced as part of God's design, not avoided as weakness. Wholeness restores what life attempted to break.

Scriptures Referenced in This Chapter

- Psalm 34:18
- Psalm 147:3
- Proverbs 4:23
- Matthew 11:28–30
- Ephesians 4:31–32
- Colossians 3:13
- Isaiah 61:1–3

Chapter 4

Physical Stewardship: Honoring the Body God Gave You

The body is often the most neglected pillar in a person's spiritual life.

Many people love God deeply, think faithfully, and care emotionally, yet treat their bodies as expendable. Rest is postponed. Nutrition is inconsistent. Movement is ignored. Sleep is sacrificed. Over time, exhaustion becomes normal, pain becomes familiar, and discipline feels impossible. People learn to push through fatigue rather than listen to it.

God never designed the body to be ignored in the pursuit of purpose.

Physical stewardship is not about appearance, comparison, or perfection. It is about honoring what God has entrusted. The body is not separate from spiritual life; it is the vessel through which spiritual life is lived. When the body is neglected, everything else eventually suffers — clarity weakens, emotions intensify, patience shortens, and faith feels heavier to carry.

Purpose requires endurance.
Endurance requires stewardship.

The Body as a Trust, Not a Tool

One of the most common misunderstandings about physical health is viewing the body as a tool to be used rather than a trust to be stewarded. When the body is treated as a tool, it is pushed until it breaks. When it is treated as a trust, it is cared for with intention.

Scripture describes the body as belonging to God. This truth reframes how physical care is understood. Stewardship implies responsibility, not ownership. It calls for wisdom, balance, and respect.

Many people unintentionally abuse their bodies in the name of responsibility. They overwork, under-rest, ignore pain, and override limits. Over time, this leads to burnout, chronic illness, emotional instability, and spiritual fatigue. None of these outcomes reflect God's design.

God values sustainability.

Why Physical Neglect Becomes Normal

Physical neglect often becomes normal because it is gradual. People do not wake up one day deciding to ignore their health. It happens slowly — one late night at a time, one skipped meal at a time, one ignored warning signal at a time.

Life becomes busy. Responsibilities multiply. Needs increase. Rest feels optional. Discipline feels inconvenient. Eventually, the body adapts to neglect, and dysfunction becomes familiar.

Many people believe they will care for their bodies "later," once life slows down. Scripture shows that life rarely slows down on its own. Stewardship must be chosen intentionally.

Ignoring the body does not increase productivity — it reduces longevity.

Rest as Physical Obedience

Rest is one of the clearest expressions of physical stewardship. Yet it is also one of the most resisted. Many people equate rest with laziness, weakness, or lack of commitment. Scripture presents rest as obedience and trust.

Rest acknowledges limitation. It recognizes that human strength is finite and that God does not require constant output to prove faithfulness. Rest is not disengagement from purpose; it is preparation for it.

God established rhythms of work and rest from the beginning. These rhythms were designed to protect the body and sustain productivity over time. When rest is ignored, the body eventually enforces it through exhaustion, illness, or injury.

A stewarded body honors rest without guilt.

Discipline Without Extremes

Physical stewardship requires discipline, but not extremes. Extremes often emerge from shame, comparison, or impatience. They create cycles of overcommitment followed by burnout.

Biblical discipline is consistent, reasonable, and sustainable. It respects the body's limits while gently strengthening it over time. Discipline rooted in stewardship seeks longevity, not quick results.

Movement, nutrition, hydration, and sleep all play roles in physical alignment. None require perfection. All require intention. Small, consistent choices shape physical health more effectively than sporadic effort.

God does not ask people to punish their bodies. He asks them to care for them.

Listening to the Body With Wisdom

The body communicates constantly. Fatigue, tension, pain, and illness are signals, not inconveniences. Ignoring these signals often leads to deeper dysfunction.

Listening to the body does not mean surrendering to discomfort. It means responding with wisdom. Sometimes the body needs rest. Sometimes it needs movement. Sometimes it needs nourishment. Discernment develops as stewardship becomes habitual.

Many people struggle to listen because they fear slowing down. They believe rest will cost them opportunities or progress. Scripture teaches that wisdom protects life. Responding to the body with care preserves capacity for purpose.

Physical Health and Emotional Stability

Physical health and emotional health are deeply connected. Exhaustion intensifies emotions. Poor nutrition affects mood. Lack of movement increases stress. When the body is depleted, emotional resilience weakens.

Many emotional struggles are compounded by physical neglect. Irritability, anxiety, and discouragement often lessen when physical care improves. This does not replace emotional healing, but it supports it.

God designed the body and emotions to function together. Stewarding one strengthens the other.

Physical Stewardship in Seasons of Limitation

Not every season allows the same level of physical activity or control. Illness, injury, age, caregiving, and demanding responsibilities all affect physical capacity. Stewardship adjusts to season.

Honoring the body does not mean forcing it beyond its limits. It means caring for it appropriately in each stage of life. God does not compare seasons; He meets people where they are.

Stewardship during limitation may look like rest instead of effort, patience instead of progress, and acceptance instead of frustration. These choices honor God just as much as active discipline.

Food, Nourishment, and Respect

Food is another area where stewardship is often misunderstood. Scripture does not promote restriction rooted in shame, nor indulgence rooted in disregard. It promotes moderation, gratitude, and wisdom.

Food nourishes the body and affects energy, focus, and health. Stewardship involves awareness rather than obsession. It is choosing nourishment over neglect, not perfection over peace.

Gratitude restores balance to physical care. When food is received as provision rather than comfort or control, stewardship becomes simpler and healthier.

Endurance Requires Care

Purpose is rarely fulfilled quickly. It unfolds over time, requiring endurance, consistency, and strength. Physical neglect shortens endurance. Stewardship extends it.

Many people burn out spiritually not because their calling is too heavy, but because their bodies are too depleted. God never intended purpose to destroy health. He intended health to support purpose.

Caring for the body is not selfish. It is strategic.

Living in Physical Alignment

Physical stewardship becomes sustainable when it is integrated into daily life rather than treated as an extra task. It is choosing rhythms that support health instead of fighting them. It is honoring limits instead of resenting them.

When the body is stewarded:

- energy stabilizes
- patience increases
- clarity improves
- endurance strengthens

The body becomes a support rather than a hindrance to purpose.

God does not ask people to offer Him broken vessels. He invites them to steward what He has given so they can live **Aligned for Purpose** with strength, clarity, and longevity.

Scriptures Referenced in This Chapter

- 1 Corinthians 6:19–20
- Romans 12:1
- Psalm 127:2
- Exodus 20:8–11
- Isaiah 40:29–31
- 3 John 1:2

Chapter 5

Financial Responsibility: Stewardship Without Fear or Shame

Money is one of the most emotionally charged subjects in a person's life. It influences security, opportunity, stress levels, relationships, confidence, and even faith. Yet for many believers, finances are an area filled with confusion, guilt, fear, or avoidance. People pray faithfully, serve diligently, and trust God sincerely, yet feel constantly strained, reactive, or ashamed when it comes to money.

God never intended finances to be a source of bondage.

Financial responsibility, when understood biblically, is not about wealth, status, or comparison. It is about **stewardship** — managing what God has entrusted with wisdom, discipline, and peace. Money itself is not the problem. The problem arises when money is handled without alignment, clarity, or purpose.

A life aligned for purpose cannot ignore finances, because finances affect nearly every other pillar. Financial stress intensifies mental strain, emotional instability, physical exhaustion, and spiritual distraction. Conversely, financial stewardship supports peace, endurance, generosity, and freedom.

God's design for money was never fear-driven survival.
It was provision, order, and trust.

Money as a Stewardship, Not an Identity

One of the greatest distortions surrounding money is identity attachment. Many people unknowingly tie their worth to their financial status. When money is abundant, confidence rises. When money is scarce, shame follows. Over time, finances begin to define self-worth rather than support life.

Scripture consistently separates identity from resources. A person's value is never measured by what they possess or lack. Yet culture often teaches the opposite. This conflict creates internal tension for believers who want to trust God but feel judged — by others or themselves — based on financial standing.

Stewardship reframes this completely.

Stewardship acknowledges that resources are entrusted, not owned. This perspective removes both pride and shame. Pride loses its grip because nothing belongs solely to us. Shame loses its power because lack does not define worth.

When money is viewed as stewardship:

- fear decreases
- comparison fades
- responsibility increases
- peace becomes possible

God does not evaluate faithfulness by amount — He evaluates it by obedience and wisdom.

Scarcity Mindset Versus Kingdom Trust

Many financial struggles are rooted not in numbers, but in mindset.

A scarcity mindset develops when life has repeatedly lacked stability. People who have experienced poverty, unpredictability, or loss often learn to live defensively. They expect lack, brace for crisis, and hold tightly to whatever comes. Even when income increases, fear remains.

Scarcity mindset is not greed — it is protection.

However, when scarcity mindset goes unaddressed, it creates constant anxiety. Decisions are driven by fear rather than wisdom. Generosity feels threatening. Planning feels impossible. Peace feels unreachable.

Scripture teaches a different foundation — **trust in provision** rather than control over outcomes. This does not mean ignoring responsibility or planning. It means trusting God as the ultimate source while stewarding wisely what is in hand.

Kingdom trust does not deny reality.
It refuses to let fear lead.

A financially aligned life learns how to plan without panic, give without fear, and save without obsession. Trust grows gradually as stewardship becomes consistent.

The Role of Discipline in Financial Peace

Financial peace rarely comes from income alone. Many people earn more money yet feel just as stressed — or more. Peace comes from **discipline aligned with purpose**.

Discipline is often misunderstood as restriction. Biblically, discipline is structure that protects freedom. It provides boundaries so resources are not consumed by impulse, pressure, or emotion.

Without discipline:

- spending becomes reactive
- saving feels impossible
- debt accumulates
- stress intensifies

With discipline:

- clarity increases
- decisions slow down
- resources stretch further
- peace becomes attainable

Discipline does not require perfection. It requires consistency. Small, intentional choices repeated over time reshape financial stability far more than drastic changes made briefly.

God values faithfulness in small things because small things compound.

Debt, Pressure, and Emotional Weight

Debt carries more than financial weight — it carries emotional and mental pressure. It creates urgency, limits options, and increases anxiety. Many people carry debt silently, feeling shame or embarrassment that prevents honest evaluation.

Scripture treats debt cautiously, not condemning those who carry it, but warning against its power. Debt often removes margin and creates dependence on future income that is not guaranteed.

Financial alignment does not shame those in debt.
It seeks freedom from its grip.

Freedom begins with honesty — acknowledging the full picture without judgment. From there, wisdom can guide gradual steps toward stability. God works through process, not panic. Sustainable progress matters more than quick relief.

Debt does not disqualify purpose.
But unmanaged debt can distract from it.

Provision Does Not Eliminate Responsibility

One of the most common misconceptions in faith is the belief that trusting God for provision removes the need for planning. Scripture never supports this idea. God provides, but He also calls for stewardship.

Provision and responsibility are not opposites — they work together.

God provided manna, but instructed boundaries.
God provided abundance, but required management.
God provides opportunity, but expects wisdom.

A financially aligned life prays for provision while practicing responsibility. It understands that faith does not replace action; it informs it. Trust without wisdom creates chaos. Wisdom without trust creates fear. Alignment requires both.

Generosity Without Guilt or Pressure

Generosity is a central biblical principle, but it is often taught in ways that produce guilt rather than freedom. Many people give out of obligation, fear, or pressure instead of joy and conviction. Over time, this creates resentment rather than gratitude.

Scripture teaches generosity as an overflow, not a burden. It is an expression of trust, not a transaction. God does not ask people to give what they do not have. He asks them to give with willing hearts.

Generosity looks different in different seasons. For some, it is financial. For others, it is time, skill, service, or support. God honors generosity that aligns with capacity and season.

A financially aligned life gives thoughtfully, not impulsively. It understands that generosity and stewardship must coexist. One should not destroy the other.

Financial Boundaries and Saying No

Many financial struggles come from an inability to say no. Pressure from family, friends, expectations, or guilt often leads people to overextend themselves. Over time, resentment grows and stability weakens.

Boundaries are an essential part of financial health.

Jesus modeled boundaries even in compassion. He did not meet every need presented to Him. He responded according to assignment, not pressure. Financial boundaries function the same way.

Saying no does not mean lack of compassion.
It means honoring responsibility.

Financial alignment includes wisdom in helping others without harming oneself. God does not ask people to rescue everyone — He asks them to steward wisely what they are given.

Money and Emotional Healing

Money often attaches itself to emotional wounds. Spending can become comfort. Saving can become control. Giving can become validation. Without awareness, financial behavior becomes emotional regulation.

Emotional healing supports financial healing.

When wounds are addressed, spending patterns stabilize. Impulses lessen. Fear loses its grip. Decisions become clearer. Financial stewardship improves not because income changes, but because emotional alignment does.

God heals holistically. Financial freedom often requires emotional restoration.

Planning for the Future Without Fear

Planning is not a lack of faith — it is an expression of wisdom. Scripture honors preparation, foresight, and intentionality. Planning acknowledges responsibility without surrendering trust.

A financially aligned life plans realistically, not obsessively. It prepares for the future without fearing it. Planning creates margin, and margin creates peace.

When finances are ordered:

- stress decreases
- choices increase
- generosity becomes sustainable
- purpose becomes less burdened

God's desire is not that people live paycheck to paycheck in constant fear. His desire is peace rooted in trust and wisdom.

Financial Stewardship and Purpose

Purpose requires resources — not extravagance, but stability. Financial chaos drains energy that could be used for calling. Stewardship restores focus.

God does not need wealth to fulfill purpose, but He honors order. When finances are aligned, they support rather than distract from what God is doing.

Financial responsibility does not guarantee ease. It creates sustainability.

Living Financially Aligned

Living financially aligned means money no longer controls emotions, identity, or peace. It becomes a tool rather than a master. It is stewarded with wisdom, humility, and trust.

When finances are aligned:

- fear loosens its grip
- generosity becomes joyful
- peace increases
- purpose gains support

God's desire is not financial stress disguised as faith.
It is stewardship rooted in trust.

To live **Aligned for Purpose**, finances must be brought under God's design — not ruled by fear, shame, or pressure, but guided by wisdom, discipline, and peace.

Scriptures Referenced in This Chapter

- Matthew 6:19–21
- Matthew 6:24–34
- Luke 16:10–13
- Proverbs 3:9–10
- Proverbs 21:5
- 1 Timothy 6:6–10
- Hebrews 13:5
- Malachi 3:10

Chapter 6

Integration: Living an Aligned Life Without Fragmentation

Alignment is not achieved by mastering one area of life while neglecting the others. True alignment happens when the spiritual, mental, emotional, physical, and financial pillars work together in harmony. This is where many people struggle — not because they lack effort, but because life has taught them to operate in fragments.

People learn to compartmentalize.
Faith stays spiritual.
Thoughts stay mental.
Emotions stay hidden.
Health gets postponed.
Money becomes stressful.

God never designed life to be lived this way.

An aligned life is an **integrated life** — one where each pillar supports the others rather than competing with them. When integration is missing, people feel stretched thin even when they are doing "everything right." When integration is present, life gains flow, stability, and sustainability.

Purpose is not lived in pieces.
It is lived in alignment.

Why Fragmentation Feels Normal

Fragmentation often feels normal because it is learned early. People are taught to address problems individually rather than holistically. If stress increases, they work harder. If emotions surface, they suppress them. If finances strain, they panic. Each response happens in isolation, without recognizing how deeply connected these areas truly are.

Life pressure reinforces fragmentation. Urgency forces people to focus on whatever feels most demanding in the moment. Over time, this creates imbalance. One area becomes dominant while others weaken.

Scripture consistently presents a different picture — one of wholeness. God addresses the heart, the mind, the body, and daily living together. Separation may feel efficient, but it is never sustainable.

Integration restores order.

How the Five Pillars Support One Another

Each pillar of the Godly Framework strengthens the others. None exist independently.

A strong **spiritual foundation** stabilizes the mind. When trust in God is present, mental anxiety loses power. Decisions slow down. Fear quiets.

A renewed **mind** supports emotional health. Clear thinking reduces emotional overreaction. Truth interrupts old patterns. Perspective replaces panic.

Healed **emotions** protect physical health. Stress lessens. The body relaxes. Energy improves. Boundaries become possible.

Healthy **physical stewardship** increases mental clarity and emotional resilience. Rest improves focus. Strength increases patience.

Wise **financial stewardship** reduces chronic stress, allowing spiritual focus, emotional peace, and physical stability to grow.

When one pillar weakens, the others feel the strain. When one pillar strengthens, the others benefit.

This is why alignment cannot be partial.

Recognizing Imbalance Without Shame

One of the greatest obstacles to integration is shame. Many people recognize imbalance but avoid addressing it because they feel embarrassed or overwhelmed. Shame keeps people stuck by convincing them they should already have it together.

God never uses shame to produce growth.

Integration begins with honest recognition. Which areas feel strained? Which feel neglected? Which feel overburdened? Awareness invites alignment. Denial delays it.

Growth does not require fixing everything at once. It requires **intentional attention**.

God works progressively. He restores order step by step.

The Role of Rhythm in an Aligned Life

Integration requires rhythm.

Rhythm is different from routine. Routine can become rigid. Rhythm adapts to season. God designed life to function in rhythms — work and rest, sowing and reaping, action and stillness.

When rhythm is ignored, imbalance grows. People overwork spiritually, mentally, emotionally, physically, or financially until exhaustion sets in. Rhythm restores sustainability.

An aligned life recognizes when to push and when to pause. It honors limits without guilt. It allows margin for restoration.

Purpose flourishes in rhythm, not in constant motion.

Alignment During Stressful Seasons

Stressful seasons reveal whether integration exists. Pressure exposes fragmentation quickly. When life intensifies, people often abandon balance to survive. Spiritual habits weaken. Mental discipline slips. Emotional health deteriorates. Physical care is ignored. Financial decisions become reactive.

Integration during stress does not eliminate difficulty — it stabilizes response.

An aligned life may still feel stretched, but it does not collapse. Each pillar provides support when another feels strained. This shared load prevents burnout.

God does not promise stress-free living. He provides **ordered living** within stress.

Boundaries as a Tool for Integration

Boundaries protect integration.

Without boundaries, one area will always dominate the others. Work consumes rest. Service consumes health. Giving consumes stability. Boundaries create balance.

Boundaries are not rejection.
They are alignment.

Jesus modeled boundaries consistently. He withdrew, rested, declined demands, and stayed focused on assignment. Boundaries preserved His effectiveness.

An integrated life uses boundaries to protect rhythm, health, peace, and purpose.

Avoiding the Trap of Perfectionism

Many people abandon integration because they believe they must maintain perfect balance at all times. This expectation is unrealistic and discouraging.

Alignment is not perfection.
It is direction.

Some seasons emphasize one pillar more than others. Integration means the other pillars are not abandoned entirely. They are supported at appropriate levels.

God values faithfulness, not flawlessness.

Integration and Identity

Identity plays a critical role in alignment. When identity is fragmented, life becomes fragmented. People define themselves by roles — worker, caregiver, provider, helper — rather than by wholeness.

Scripture presents identity as unified. A person is not multiple selves; they are one person living many expressions.

Integration restores identity. It allows people to live consistently across settings — spiritually grounded, mentally clear, emotionally healthy, physically cared for, and financially responsible.

This consistency brings peace.

Integration Strengthens Endurance

Endurance is required for purpose. Purpose unfolds over time, often through adversity, delay, and responsibility. Fragmentation weakens endurance. Integration strengthens it. An integrated life recovers faster from stress. It adapts more easily to change. It sustains commitment without resentment.

God designed alignment to protect longevity.

Living Aligned in Ordinary Life

Integration is practiced in ordinary moments — not dramatic decisions.

Choosing rest before exhaustion.
Pausing before reacting.
Planning before spending.
Processing emotions honestly.
Praying before acting.

These small choices compound into stability.

An aligned life feels less frantic, even when busy. Peace becomes accessible. Clarity increases. Purpose feels supported rather than strained.

Alignment Is a Daily Practice

Alignment is not a one-time achievement. It is a daily practice of awareness, adjustment, and trust. Some days require correction. Others require rest. God's grace supports both.

Living aligned does not mean life becomes easy. It means life becomes **ordered**.

Order creates peace.
Peace sustains purpose.

The Outcome of an Aligned Life

When life is integrated:

- faith feels lived, not compartmentalized
- decisions feel intentional, not rushed
- emotions feel processed, not suppressed
- the body feels supported, not ignored
- finances feel stewarded, not feared

This is the life God designed — not fragmented, not frantic, not fear-driven. It is a life **Aligned for Purpose**.

Scriptures Referenced in This Chapter

- Mark 12:30
- Proverbs 4:23–27
- Ecclesiastes 3:1–8
- 1 Thessalonians 5:23
- Colossians 3:15–17
- Psalm 37:23–24

Chapter 7

Mental Renewal: Understanding the Battlefield of the Mind

Every life is shaped first in the mind.

Long before decisions are made, actions taken, or words spoken, thoughts are formed. These thoughts quietly influence perception, shape emotional responses, and determine behavior. Many people focus on changing outcomes without realizing that the true battleground lies beneath the surface — in the patterns of the mind.

God designed the mind to be a place of clarity, wisdom, and discernment. Yet for many, the mind has become a place of noise, fear, confusion, and exhaustion. Thoughts run unchecked. Worries repeat. Regret lingers. Fear predicts outcomes that may never come. Even people with deep faith often struggle mentally, wondering why belief has not brought rest.

Mental struggle is not spiritual failure.
It is a signal that renewal is needed.

Mental renewal is the second pillar of an aligned life because without it, every other area suffers. A misaligned mind distorts faith, intensifies emotion, weakens discipline, and fuels fear around provision. God's design includes a renewed mind because purpose cannot be sustained by a mind trapped in old patterns.

Why the Mind Becomes a Battlefield

The mind becomes a battlefield because it is where interpretation happens. Life events do not automatically determine meaning — the mind assigns meaning to them. Two people can experience the same situation and respond completely differently based on how their minds interpret it.

Past experiences, trauma, environment, and repeated exposure shape mental responses. Over time, the mind develops shortcuts — automatic thoughts that attempt to protect or prepare. These shortcuts often originate in survival, not truth.

When life has been unpredictable, the mind learns to expect instability.
When loss has been repeated, the mind learns to anticipate disappointment.
When rejection has occurred, the mind learns to guard against vulnerability.

These patterns are learned, not chosen — but they can be renewed.

God does not condemn people for mental struggle. He invites transformation.

The Power of Repetition

The mind is shaped by repetition. Thoughts that are repeated become beliefs. Beliefs shape identity. Identity shapes behavior. This process happens quietly and consistently.

Many people unknowingly repeat thoughts that undermine peace:

- "I'm always behind."
- "Something is about to go wrong."
- "I can't afford to make a mistake."

- "I'm not good at this."
- "I'll never catch up."

These thoughts may feel realistic because they are familiar, not because they are true. Familiarity often masquerades as truth in the mind.

Mental renewal requires interrupting repetition. It requires noticing thought patterns and questioning whether they align with truth or fear. This process is uncomfortable at first because the mind resists change. However, consistency reshapes mental pathways over time.

God designed the mind to be transformed, not trapped.

Thoughts Versus Identity

One of the most damaging misunderstandings about the mind is the belief that thoughts define identity. Many people assume that because a thought appears, it must represent who they are.

This belief creates shame and confusion.

Thoughts are experiences — not identity statements. They arise from memory, emotion, environment, and habit. They do not automatically reflect truth or character.

Mental renewal teaches discernment between *having* a thought and *agreeing* with it. Agreement gives a thought power. Discernment removes it.

God does not hold people accountable for intrusive or uninvited thoughts. He invites them to bring those thoughts into alignment with truth.

Identity is not formed by mental noise.
It is anchored in relationship with God.

Fear-Based Thinking and Its Effects

Fear is one of the most influential forces in the mind. It narrows perspective, accelerates urgency, and distorts judgment. Fear-based thinking often disguises itself as responsibility, realism, or caution.

Fear says:

- "Prepare for the worst."
- "You can't trust this."
- "You need control to stay safe."
- "If you stop, everything will fall apart."

While fear feels protective, it exhausts the mind and undermines peace. It creates constant mental scanning for threats that may never appear.

Scripture addresses fear repeatedly because fear weakens trust. Mental renewal does not eliminate caution; it removes panic. It teaches the mind how to remain alert without becoming overwhelmed.

A renewed mind learns to respond rather than react.

Anxiety and Overthinking

Anxiety is often the result of unresolved mental loops. The mind replays possibilities, regrets, or imagined futures in an attempt to prevent harm. Unfortunately, this only amplifies stress.

Overthinking is not wisdom — it is mental overload.

Many people believe if they think long enough, they can control outcomes. Scripture teaches a different approach — trust paired with wisdom. God never asked the mind to carry every possible outcome. He asked it to walk daily in alignment.

Mental renewal creates space. It teaches the mind when to engage and when to release. Peace does not come from solving every possibility; it comes from trusting God with what cannot be controlled.

Mental Discipline Without Harshness

Mental discipline is often misunderstood as harsh self-control or suppression. Biblical discipline is different. It is gentle, intentional redirection toward truth.

A renewed mind does not punish itself for negative thoughts. It notices them, evaluates them, and replaces them. Shame undermines renewal. Grace supports it.

God's patience with the renewal process reflects His understanding of how deeply ingrained patterns can be. Change is expected to be gradual.

Mental discipline becomes sustainable when it is rooted in compassion rather than criticism.

The Role of Scripture in Mental Alignment

Scripture provides a stable reference point for the mind. It anchors thoughts in truth that does not shift with emotion or circumstance. When Scripture is internalized, it becomes a filter through which thoughts are evaluated.

This does not happen instantly. It develops as Scripture is applied to real situations repeatedly. Over time, truth begins to surface naturally in moments of pressure.

A renewed mind does not quote Scripture mechanically — it lives it instinctively.

Scripture does not silence the mind.
It steadies it.

Rest and the Renewed Mind

Rest is essential to mental renewal. A fatigued mind is vulnerable to fear, distortion, and emotional overwhelm. God designed rest to restore clarity.

Many people resist rest because they fear falling behind. Scripture presents rest as trust — the belief that life will not collapse if productivity pauses.

Mental clarity often returns in rest. Answers surface when striving stops. Renewal accelerates when the mind is given space to breathe.

Rest is not avoidance.
It is alignment.

Mental Renewal in Daily Life

Mental renewal is practiced in ordinary moments:

- pausing before reacting
- questioning fearful assumptions
- choosing prayer over panic
- replacing lies with truth
- allowing rest without guilt

These small choices reshape the mind gradually. Over time, thoughts slow, clarity increases, and peace becomes accessible.

A renewed mind does not eliminate difficulty — it transforms response.

How Mental Renewal Supports Purpose

Purpose requires clarity. A misaligned mind distorts calling, weakens confidence, and drains energy. A renewed mind supports endurance, wisdom, and courage. When the mind is aligned:

- fear loses influence
- decisions become clearer
- emotions stabilize
- faith feels steady

Mental renewal restores authority over thought life rather than allowing thought life to control direction.

God's design is not mental survival.
It is mental freedom.

To live **Aligned for Purpose**, the mind must be renewed consistently, patiently, and intentionally. This renewal supports every other pillar and strengthens the foundation for a life lived with clarity and peace.

Scriptures Referenced in This Chapter

- Romans 12:2
- Proverbs 4:23
- Isaiah 26:3
- Philippians 4:6–8
- 2 Corinthians 10:3–5
- Psalm 139:23–24
- James 1:5

Chapter 8

Emotional Resilience: Remaining Steady When Life Is Unstable

Emotional resilience is not the absence of pain.
It is the ability to remain steady when pain arrives.

Life does not move in straight lines. It shifts, interrupts, disappoints, and challenges even the most faithful people. Loss happens. Plans change. People fail. Expectations collapse. In these moments, emotional resilience determines whether a person breaks down or bends without breaking.

Many people mistake emotional resilience for emotional hardness. They believe strength means suppressing feelings, staying silent, or pushing through without processing pain. God's design is different. Emotional resilience is not numbness — it is **regulated strength**. It is the capacity to experience emotion without being consumed by it.

An aligned life requires emotional resilience because purpose unfolds in imperfect conditions. Without resilience, emotions dictate decisions. With resilience, emotions inform wisdom without controlling direction.

Why Emotional Instability Develops

Emotional instability does not usually come from weakness. It often comes from **unprocessed experience.**

People endure seasons of survival where emotions must be set aside to function. They stay strong for children, family, work, or crisis. Over time, unprocessed emotions accumulate beneath the surface. Eventually, pressure exposes what was never healed.

Instability appears as:

- overreaction to small triggers
- emotional numbness
- chronic irritability
- fear of conflict
- avoidance of vulnerability
- emotional exhaustion

These responses are not moral failures. They are signs that emotional capacity has been exceeded.

God never intended people to live indefinitely in survival mode.

Resilience Begins With Emotional Awareness

Resilience begins by recognizing what is happening internally without judgment. Many people feel emotions before they understand them. They react before they reflect. Emotional awareness slows the process.

Awareness asks:

- What am I feeling?
- Why does this feel intense?
- What experience is this connected to?
- What belief is being activated?

These questions create space between feeling and reaction. That space is where resilience develops.

Scripture consistently invites reflection rather than impulsive reaction. Emotional awareness allows emotions to be acknowledged without allowing them to take control.

What is acknowledged can be processed.
What is denied gains power.

Regulation Over Suppression

Emotional resilience depends on regulation, not suppression.

Suppression ignores emotion. Regulation manages it. Suppressed emotions resurface later — often intensified and misplaced. Regulated emotions are felt, named, and released appropriately.

God designed emotions to signal information, not to dictate behavior. Resilience forms when a person learns how to sit with emotion long enough to understand it, but not long enough to be overwhelmed by it.

This takes practice. Emotional regulation is learned, not automatic. It requires patience, grace, and consistency.

God is patient in this process.

Triggers and Emotional Memory

Emotional triggers are responses to present situations that are connected to past experiences. A reaction feels disproportionate because it is layered — the present moment awakens unresolved memory.

Triggers are not signs of immaturity. They are invitations to healing.

Resilient people do not avoid triggers forever. They learn from them. They ask what memory is being activated and what belief is surfacing. Over time, triggers lose their intensity as healing progresses.

God does not shame emotional reactions. He uses them to reveal areas that still need care.

Resilience and Boundaries

Boundaries play a critical role in emotional resilience. Without boundaries, emotional capacity is constantly drained. People become overwhelmed not because they care too much, but because they care without limits.

Resilience requires discernment:

- knowing when to engage
- knowing when to rest
- knowing when to say no
- knowing when to step back

Jesus modeled emotional boundaries consistently. He loved deeply without absorbing every demand. He withdrew when needed. He protected His emotional capacity to remain effective.

Boundaries preserve resilience.
Without them, burnout is inevitable.

Responding Instead of Reacting

One of the clearest signs of emotional resilience is the ability to respond rather than react. Reaction is immediate and emotional. Response is thoughtful and intentional.

Reaction seeks relief.
Response seeks alignment.

Resilience allows a pause between emotion and action. That pause changes outcomes. It prevents regret, preserves relationships, and protects peace.

Scripture consistently emphasizes self-control — not as suppression, but as strength. Emotional resilience grows as responses become slower, calmer, and wiser.

Resilience in Relationships

Relationships test emotional resilience more than any other area of life. Misunderstanding, disappointment, conflict, and unmet expectations expose emotional limits quickly.

Without resilience:

- conflict feels threatening
- disagreement feels personal
- withdrawal feels safer than engagement

With resilience:

- communication improves
- conflict becomes manageable
- trust rebuilds gradually

Resilient people do not avoid relationships. They navigate them with wisdom. They understand that emotional safety requires honesty, boundaries, and grace — not perfection.

Grief, Loss, and Endurance

Grief is one of the greatest tests of emotional resilience. Loss disrupts identity, routine, and expectation. Many people rush grief because they fear being overwhelmed by it.

Scripture allows space for grief. It does not demand quick recovery. Emotional resilience honors grief without allowing it to define the future.

Endurance develops when grief is processed rather than avoided. Healing does not erase loss — it integrates it into life with meaning.

God meets people in grief, not after it.

Resilience Is Built Over Time

Emotional resilience is not a personality trait. It is a capacity built through experience, reflection, and healing. Each time a person processes emotion rather than reacting impulsively, resilience strengthens.

Each time a boundary is honored, capacity increases.
Each time truth replaces fear, stability grows.

God values progress over speed.

Emotional Resilience Supports Purpose

Purpose requires endurance. Endurance requires emotional resilience. Without it, people abandon calling prematurely or carry it resentfully.

Emotionally resilient people remain steady in adversity. They recover faster from disappointment. They adapt without losing identity.

Resilience does not eliminate emotion — it harnesses it.

Living With Emotional Strength

Living emotionally resilient does not mean never struggling. It means knowing how to navigate struggle without losing alignment. It means emotions no longer control direction.

When emotional resilience is present:

- reactions soften
- peace increases
- clarity improves
- relationships strengthen

God's desire is not emotional survival.
It is emotional strength rooted in wisdom.

To live **Aligned for Purpose**, emotional resilience must be cultivated intentionally. It protects peace, sustains relationships, and supports endurance through every season of life.

Scriptures Referenced in This Chapter

- Proverbs 16:32
- Psalm 42:5
- Ecclesiastes 3:4
- John 14:27
- Galatians 5:22–23
- Isaiah 43:2
- 2 Corinthians 4:16–18

Chapter 9

Emotional Healing in Relationships: Restoring Trust Without Losing Yourself

Relationships are where emotional wounds are most often formed — and where they are most clearly revealed.

People can manage their emotions in isolation, appear composed in public, and remain productive in responsibility, yet find themselves unraveling in close relationships. Familiar patterns resurface. Old fears awaken. Defenses rise. Reactions feel stronger than expected. Words spoken long ago echo louder than present reality.

This is not accidental.

God designed relationships to be places of connection, growth, and reflection. They reveal what still needs healing. They expose beliefs formed in earlier seasons. They test emotional maturity in ways solitude never can. For many people, unresolved emotional wounds do not become visible until intimacy is required.

Emotional healing in relationships is not about becoming detached or guarded. It is about learning how to remain open without becoming unprotected, how to trust without abandoning discernment, and how to love without losing identity.

An aligned life requires healed relationships because purpose is rarely fulfilled alone.

Why Relationships Trigger Emotional Wounds

Relationships trigger emotional wounds because they activate memory. The heart remembers experiences the mind has learned to minimize. Tone, absence, rejection, conflict, or inconsistency can awaken emotions rooted in earlier relationships — parents, caregivers, partners, authority figures, or formative friendships.

Many reactions in present relationships are responses to past pain.

A delayed reply feels like abandonment.
Disagreement feels like rejection.
Distance feels like loss.

These reactions are often disproportionate to the present moment because they are layered with unresolved experience. Emotional healing requires recognizing this layering rather than judging it.

God does not shame emotional reactions. He uses them to reveal where healing is still needed.

Attachment, Trust, and Emotional Safety

Trust develops through emotional safety. When safety has been broken repeatedly, the heart learns to protect itself. This protection can appear as withdrawal, hyper-independence, control, people-pleasing, or emotional shutdown.

These patterns are not flaws. They are adaptations.

However, what once protected the heart can later prevent intimacy. Emotional healing involves gently dismantling defenses that no longer serve the present season. This process cannot be rushed, because trust rebuilds gradually.

God's approach to healing is patient. He restores trust layer by layer, allowing the heart to relearn safety without forcing vulnerability.

Communication and Emotional Honesty

Many relational wounds persist not because of what happened, but because of what was never expressed. Unspoken emotions accumulate. Assumptions replace conversation. Silence becomes safer than honesty.

Emotional healing requires learning how to communicate truthfully without aggression or fear. This does not mean oversharing or emotional dumping. It means expressing feelings responsibly, with clarity and respect.

Healthy communication acknowledges emotion without assigning blame. It creates space for understanding rather than defense. When communication improves, relationships often soften.

God values truth spoken in love because truth without love wounds, and love without truth confuses.

Forgiveness Within Relationships

Forgiveness is essential to relational healing, yet it is often misunderstood. Forgiveness does not deny harm or require immediate reconciliation. It releases emotional debt so healing can begin.

Holding resentment keeps wounds active. Forgiveness interrupts the cycle of re-injury by freeing the heart from constant replay. This process is often gradual. Forgiveness may need to be chosen repeatedly before emotional relief settles fully.

God does not demand forgiveness to benefit the offender. He invites forgiveness to heal the wounded.

Forgiveness restores emotional freedom, not relational obligation.

Boundaries as an Act of Love

Boundaries are often misunderstood as rejection. In truth, boundaries protect connection. Without them, relationships become unsafe, resentful, or draining.

Emotional healing includes learning where responsibility ends and where another person's begins. Boundaries clarify expectations, protect emotional energy, and create space for healthier interaction.

Jesus demonstrated boundaries consistently. He loved deeply without allowing constant access. He withdrew when necessary. He did not explain Himself to everyone. His boundaries preserved His capacity to love well.

Boundaries do not limit love.
They sustain it.

Healing Relationship Patterns

Many people repeat relational patterns without understanding why. They attract similar dynamics, experience similar conflicts, and feel familiar disappointments. Patterns persist until awareness interrupts them.

Emotional healing involves identifying patterns honestly:
Why do certain conflicts repeat?
Why does distance feel threatening?
Why does closeness feel unsafe?
Why does approval feel necessary?

These questions reveal beliefs formed in earlier relationships. Healing occurs when beliefs are replaced with truth and new responses are practiced intentionally.

God does not condemn repeated patterns. He invites transformation through awareness and patience.

Emotional Independence and Interdependence

Emotional healing restores balance between independence and connection. Some people over-attach emotionally, losing themselves in relationships. Others over-detach, avoiding vulnerability entirely.

God's design is interdependence — connection without loss of self.

A healed emotional life allows closeness without fear and independence without isolation. It respects individuality while honoring connection.

This balance supports healthy relationships and prevents emotional burnout.

Conflict as a Tool for Growth

Conflict is unavoidable in meaningful relationships. Emotional healing changes how conflict is interpreted. Rather than seeing conflict as threat, healed individuals view it as information.

Conflict reveals expectations, boundaries, needs, and misalignment. When handled with emotional maturity, conflict strengthens trust rather than eroding it.

Avoiding conflict often prolongs emotional pain. Addressing it respectfully supports healing.

God values reconciliation rooted in truth, not avoidance rooted in fear.

Healing in Family Relationships

Family relationships often carry the deepest emotional imprint. Early experiences shape beliefs about love, safety, authority, and worth. Emotional healing within family dynamics can be complex and slow.

Healing does not always result in restored closeness. Sometimes it results in peace, clarity, and acceptance. God honors healing in all forms, not only reconciliation.

Emotional wholeness allows individuals to relate to family with wisdom rather than obligation, compassion rather than resentment.

Romantic Relationships and Emotional Healing

Romantic relationships often intensify emotional wounds because of vulnerability and expectation. Emotional healing allows love without dependency and commitment without fear.

Healed individuals choose partners from alignment rather than need. They communicate openly, set boundaries confidently, and address issues without avoidance.

God desires relationships that reflect security, respect, and mutual growth.

Healing Requires Time and Grace

Relational healing does not happen quickly because trust is rebuilt gradually. Setbacks may occur. Old reactions may resurface. Progress may feel uneven.

God's grace covers the process.

Healing is measured not by perfection, but by increased awareness, healthier responses, and growing peace.

Emotionally Healed Relationships Support Purpose

Purpose flourishes in healthy relationships. Emotional healing reduces distraction, restores energy, and strengthens support systems.

When relationships heal:

- peace increases
- communication improves
- trust rebuilds
- emotional strength grows

God designed relationships to support purpose, not sabotage it.

Living Relationally Aligned

Living relationally aligned means engaging relationships with honesty, wisdom, and emotional maturity. It means loving without fear, forgiving without denial, and setting boundaries without guilt.

God does not want His people relationally wounded and isolated. He wants them healed, connected, and supported.

To live **Aligned for Purpose**, emotional healing within relationships must be embraced intentionally. It restores trust, strengthens connection, and allows love to function without fear.

Scriptures Referenced in This Chapter

- Proverbs 17:17
- Proverbs 18:24
- Matthew 18:15
- Ephesians 4:2–3
- Colossians 3:12–14
- Romans 12:18
- Psalm 133:1

Chapter 10

Emotional Freedom: Releasing the Past Without Carrying It Forward

Emotional freedom is not forgetting the past.
It is learning how to live without being controlled by it.

Many people believe they have moved on because time has passed. They no longer speak about what hurt them. They function, adapt, and press forward. Yet beneath the surface, old experiences continue to shape reactions, decisions, relationships, and expectations. The past may no longer be visible, but it remains influential.

God never intended healing to mean silent endurance.

Emotional freedom is not denial. It is release. It is the process of allowing God to heal wounds deeply enough that they no longer dictate the future. When emotional freedom is absent, people unknowingly relive the same patterns in new environments. When emotional freedom is present, life begins to feel lighter, clearer, and less reactive.

An aligned life requires emotional freedom because purpose cannot flourish where the past still rules.

How the Past Continues to Influence the Present

The past influences the present not because people choose it, but because memory shapes perception. Experiences form expectations.

Pain teaches caution. Loss teaches restraint. Betrayal teaches distance. Over time, these lessons become internal rules that guide behavior.

People may say they are fine, yet:
They expect disappointment before it arrives.
They withdraw before rejection happens.
They over-control to avoid uncertainty.
They avoid vulnerability to prevent pain.

These behaviors feel protective, but they are often prisons built from old wounds.

God does not blame people for these responses. He understands how deeply pain imprints the heart. Emotional freedom begins with recognizing how much influence the past still holds.

Awareness does not reopen wounds.
It exposes what needs healing.

When Survival Becomes a Lifestyle

Many emotional patterns originate in survival seasons. During hardship, people learn to adapt quickly. They become strong, independent, guarded, or hyper-aware. These adaptations are necessary in crisis, but dangerous when carried forward indefinitely.

Survival mode keeps people alert but exhausted. It prioritizes protection over connection. It values control over trust. Even when danger passes, the nervous system may remain on high alert.

Emotional freedom requires transitioning from survival to safety.

God does not want His people permanently braced for impact. He invites them into rest, trust, and restoration. This transition takes time because the body and emotions must relearn safety.

Healing does not mean the past was insignificant.
It means it no longer defines the present.

Unspoken Pain and Emotional Weight

Some of the heaviest emotional burdens are unspoken. Pain that was never acknowledged becomes internalized. People move on externally while carrying unresolved grief, anger, disappointment, or shame internally.

Unspoken pain does not disappear. It settles.

Over time, it manifests as:
chronic tension
emotional numbness
irritability
fatigue
difficulty trusting
difficulty receiving love

God invites honesty because healing requires truth. Emotional freedom begins when pain is named rather than buried. Scripture consistently shows people bringing their pain to God openly — not with polished words, but with honesty.

God meets people where they are, not where they pretend to be.

Shame and Its Grip on the Heart

Shame is one of the strongest forces preventing emotional freedom. Shame convinces people that their pain is a personal failure rather than a response to experience. It keeps wounds hidden and reinforces isolation.

Shame says:
"I should be over this."
"I shouldn't feel this way."
"Something is wrong with me."

God never speaks through shame. Scripture consistently separates identity from experience. Pain does not define worth. Trauma does not erase value. Failure does not cancel calling.

Emotional freedom grows as shame loses its authority. This happens when truth replaces self-condemnation and grace replaces judgment.

God heals without humiliating.

Forgiveness as Release, Not Reconciliation

Forgiveness is central to emotional freedom, yet it is often misunderstood and misapplied. Forgiveness does not require forgetting, excusing, or restoring access. It requires release.

Forgiveness is the decision to stop carrying what does not belong to you.

When forgiveness is withheld, emotional energy remains tied to the offense. Thoughts replay. Emotions resurface. The past remains active. Forgiveness interrupts this cycle by releasing the emotional hold of the experience.

Forgiveness may be a process rather than a moment. It may need to be chosen repeatedly as memories resurface. God honors each step toward release.

Forgiveness frees the wounded, not the offender.

Grief, Loss, and Emotional Completion

Grief is often unresolved because it is rushed. People are encouraged to move on quickly, stay strong, or focus forward. Yet grief demands processing. Emotional freedom requires completion.

Completion does not mean forgetting loss. It means integrating it into life without constant pain. It allows sorrow to coexist with peace and memory to coexist with hope.

God allows space for grief because He understands its depth. Emotional freedom honors grief without allowing it to dominate identity.

Healing does not erase love.
It transforms how love is carried.

Breaking Emotional Cycles

Many people unknowingly repeat emotional cycles formed in earlier seasons. They respond to current situations with old reactions. These cycles persist until awareness interrupts them.

Emotional freedom involves noticing patterns:
Why does this trigger feel familiar?
Why does this response feel automatic?
Why does this situation feel heavier than it should?

These questions lead to insight. Insight creates choice. Choice allows change.

God does not shame repetition. He invites awareness so transformation can begin.

The Role of the Mind in Emotional Freedom

Emotions and thoughts are deeply connected. Unhealed emotions often generate distorted thoughts, and distorted thoughts intensify emotion. Emotional freedom requires alignment of both.

Renewing the mind supports emotional release. Truth interrupts emotional lies formed during pain. Over time, emotional reactions soften as mental clarity increases.

God heals holistically. Emotional freedom and mental renewal work together.

Letting Go Without Losing Wisdom

One of the greatest fears surrounding emotional freedom is the belief that letting go means becoming vulnerable again. Many people fear they will repeat the same mistakes if they release caution.

Emotional freedom does not remove wisdom.
It removes fear.

Healing allows discernment to replace hyper-vigilance. It restores balance between openness and protection. A healed heart is not careless — it is confident.

God restores wisdom alongside freedom.

Freedom Does Not Mean the Absence of Memory

Emotional freedom does not erase memory. Memories may remain, but they lose emotional charge. They no longer dictate reactions or decisions. They become information rather than identity.

This shift is profound. Life becomes less reactive. Relationships feel safer. Peace becomes more consistent.

The past becomes a chapter, not a ruler.

Emotional Freedom Supports Purpose

Purpose requires emotional capacity. When emotional energy is consumed by the past, little remains for the future. Emotional freedom restores capacity.

As freedom increases:
clarity improves
relationships stabilize
energy returns
peace deepens

God desires His people to live forward, not bound by what has already passed.

Living Emotionally Free

Living emotionally free means engaging life without carrying unnecessary weight. It means responding rather than reacting, trusting rather than guarding, and moving forward without dragging the past behind.

God does not want emotional captivity disguised as strength.
He wants healing that restores joy, peace, and alignment.

To live **Aligned for Purpose**, emotional freedom must be embraced fully. It releases the past, restores the present, and makes space for a future guided by peace rather than pain.

Scriptures Referenced in This Chapter

- Isaiah 43:18–19
- Psalm 55:22
- Matthew 11:28–30
- Philippians 3:13–14
- Romans 8:1
- 2 Corinthians 5:17
- Psalm 103:12

Chapter 11

Physical Discipline: Building Strength That Sustains Purpose

Physical discipline is not about control.
It is about **capacity**.

Many people misunderstand physical discipline as restriction, punishment, or obsession. They associate it with extreme routines, unrealistic standards, or shame-based motivation. As a result, they either avoid it entirely or pursue it in unsustainable bursts. God's design for physical discipline is neither neglect nor extremism. It is stewardship that builds strength for the long haul.

Purpose is not fulfilled in short sprints.
It is carried over time.

A body that lacks discipline eventually becomes a burden rather than a support. Energy declines. Focus weakens. Recovery slows. Emotions intensify. Faith feels heavier to carry. None of this happens suddenly. It develops gradually as discipline is postponed in the name of responsibility, service, or survival.

God never intended discipline to steal joy.
He intended it to **preserve strength**.

Discipline as a Form of Respect

Physical discipline begins with respect for the body. Respect acknowledges that the body has limits, rhythms, and needs. Ignoring these realities does not demonstrate dedication — it demonstrates disregard.

Scripture presents discipline as a positive force. It is associated with training, preparation, and readiness. Discipline is what allows the body to support calling rather than compete with it. Without discipline, the body becomes reactive. With discipline, it becomes reliable.

Many people push their bodies until exhaustion and call it faithfulness. God calls it imbalance. Discipline honors the body enough to care for it intentionally rather than exploiting it until it fails.

Respect-based discipline is patient. It does not rush results or demand perfection. It focuses on consistency rather than intensity.

Why Discipline Often Feels Difficult

Discipline feels difficult because it requires saying no in a culture that rewards constant yes. It challenges habits formed through convenience, exhaustion, and survival. It asks for intentionality in a world that normalizes neglect.

Many people resist discipline because they associate it with failure. Past attempts that did not last create discouragement. Shame convinces them that if they could not maintain discipline before, they never will.

God does not view discipline as proof of worth.
He views it as an expression of wisdom.

Discipline is not a personality trait. It is a skill developed through practice. It strengthens gradually as habits replace impulse. God meets people at the starting point, not the finish line.

The Difference Between Motivation and Discipline

Motivation is emotional. Discipline is intentional.

Motivation rises and falls. It depends on mood, energy, and circumstance. Discipline remains steady regardless of how a person feels. Many people wait for motivation to care for their bodies. Discipline acts even when motivation is absent.

God designed discipline to support obedience, not emotion. Obedience does not require enthusiasm. It requires commitment.

When discipline is rooted in purpose rather than appearance, it becomes sustainable. The goal is not to look a certain way, but to live with strength, endurance, and clarity.

Training the Body for Endurance

Scripture often uses physical metaphors to describe spiritual endurance. Training implies repetition, patience, and progression. No one becomes strong by accident. Strength is built intentionally over time.

The body responds to consistent challenge and consistent care. Discipline balances effort with recovery. Without recovery, effort becomes damage. Without effort, recovery becomes stagnation.

God's design for the body includes growth through resistance. Resistance strengthens muscles, increases capacity, and improves resilience. Avoiding all discomfort weakens the body just as much as ignoring pain damages it.

Wisdom discerns the difference.

Routine as a Support, Not a Prison

Routine is one of the most effective tools for physical discipline, yet many people resist it. They fear routine will feel restrictive or boring. In reality, routine reduces decision fatigue and preserves energy.

Routine does not eliminate flexibility. It creates structure that supports consistency. A disciplined body benefits from predictable patterns of movement, nourishment, rest, and recovery.

God designed rhythms to support life. Routine honors those rhythms without demanding rigidity. When routine is interrupted, discipline returns without shame.

Consistency matters more than perfection.

Discipline and Mental Clarity

Physical discipline supports mental clarity. Movement improves focus. Strength increases confidence. Consistent care stabilizes mood. When the body is disciplined, the mind benefits.

Many people attempt to address mental fatigue without addressing physical neglect. Over time, this becomes ineffective. The body and mind function together. Discipline strengthens both.

God designed physical care to support mental renewal. A disciplined body creates an environment where clarity can grow.

Discipline Without Comparison

Comparison undermines discipline. When people measure progress against others, discouragement follows quickly. God never designed discipline to be competitive. It is personal.

Every body is different. Capacity varies by age, season, health, and responsibility. Discipline adapts to season. What matters is alignment, not comparison.

God honors faithfulness within capacity. Discipline rooted in comparison produces frustration. Discipline rooted in stewardship produces peace.

Physical Discipline During Busy Seasons

Busy seasons challenge discipline the most. Responsibilities increase. Time feels scarce. Fatigue grows. These seasons often reveal whether discipline has been integrated or treated as optional.

Discipline during busy seasons may look simpler. Shorter movement. More intentional rest. Cleaner boundaries. Discipline adapts rather than disappears.

God does not require extreme routines in demanding seasons. He requires wisdom.

Maintaining discipline during pressure preserves strength for what matters most.

Rest as Part of Discipline

Rest is not the opposite of discipline. It is part of it.

Many people believe discipline means constant effort. Scripture teaches balance. Without rest, discipline becomes destructive. Rest allows the body to recover, rebuild, and grow stronger.

Discipline without rest leads to injury, exhaustion, and burnout. God designed rest as an active component of strength-building, not a passive luxury.

A disciplined life honors rest without guilt.

Food, Fuel, and Discipline

Physical discipline includes intentional nourishment. Food fuels energy, focus, and recovery. Discipline does not demand perfection in eating — it demands awareness.

Eating driven by stress, distraction, or emotion weakens discipline. Eating with intention supports it. Gratitude restores balance to nourishment.

God provided food as sustenance, not control. Discipline brings moderation rather than obsession.

Pain, Discomfort, and Wisdom

Discipline includes learning how to differentiate between discomfort and damage. Discomfort often accompanies growth. Damage signals harm. Wisdom discerns which is which.

Ignoring pain leads to injury. Avoiding all discomfort prevents growth. Discipline listens to the body and responds appropriately.

God values wisdom over extremes.

Strength That Supports Calling

Physical discipline builds strength that supports calling. Calling requires endurance, presence, and availability. A neglected body limits capacity. A disciplined body extends it.

God does not need extraordinary strength to fulfill purpose. He honors sustainable strength.

Physical discipline does not glorify the body.
It equips it.

Living a Disciplined Physical Life

Living a disciplined physical life means caring for the body consistently, patiently, and wisely. It means building habits that support longevity rather than chasing quick change.

When physical discipline is present:
energy stabilizes
clarity improves
endurance increases
confidence strengthens

The body becomes a partner in purpose rather than an obstacle.

God designed discipline to protect purpose, not compete with it.
To live **Aligned for Purpose**, physical discipline must be embraced as stewardship that builds strength for the journey ahead.

Scriptures Referenced in This Chapter

- 1 Corinthians 9:24–27
- Hebrews 12:11
- Proverbs 12:1
- 1 Timothy 4:8
- Isaiah 40:31
- Proverbs 25:28

Chapter 12

Physical Rest and Recovery: Sustaining Purpose Without Burnout

Burnout is rarely caused by doing too much at once.
It is caused by doing too much for too long without recovery.

Many people assume burnout is a personal failure — a lack of discipline, motivation, or faith. In reality, burnout is often the result of ignoring God's design for rest. People push through fatigue, override limits, and postpone recovery in the name of responsibility, service, or urgency. Over time, exhaustion becomes normal. Weariness becomes familiar. Joy fades quietly.

God never intended purpose to be carried by depleted bodies.

Physical rest and recovery are not indulgences. They are essential components of stewardship. Without them, discipline becomes damaging rather than strengthening. With them, strength becomes sustainable.

An aligned life understands that rest does not oppose productivity — it **protects** it.

Why Rest Is Resisted

Rest is resisted because it confronts identity.

Many people tie worth to productivity. They feel valuable when they are needed, busy, or accomplishing something. Rest threatens that identity. It forces stillness where validation has been drawn from motion.

Others resist rest because of fear. They fear falling behind, disappointing others, or losing momentum. Some fear what might surface emotionally if they slow down. For those who have lived in survival mode, rest feels unsafe.

Scripture presents rest as trust.
To rest is to believe that God is still at work when we stop.

God established rest as a rhythm, not a reward. From the beginning, rest was woven into creation. It was not introduced after exhaustion — it was designed to prevent it.

Rest Is Not Laziness

One of the greatest misconceptions about rest is equating it with laziness. Laziness avoids responsibility. Rest prepares for it. Laziness neglects purpose. Rest sustains it.

Scripture consistently distinguishes between the two. God honors diligence, but He also commands rest. Ignoring rest does not demonstrate devotion — it demonstrates imbalance.

Jesus rested.

He withdrew from crowds.
He stepped away from demand.
He slept when exhausted.

His rest did not weaken His purpose. It strengthened it.

A life aligned with God's design does not glorify exhaustion. It honors sustainability.

The Cost of Ignoring Recovery

When recovery is ignored, the body enforces it eventually. Fatigue turns into illness. Stress turns into injury. Overextension turns into breakdown. These outcomes are not punishments — they are signals.

Ignoring these signals creates long-term consequences:
chronic exhaustion
weakened immunity
mental fog
emotional volatility
spiritual dullness

Many people attempt to address these symptoms individually without addressing the root cause: a lack of intentional recovery.

God designed the body to heal, but healing requires space.

Rest as an Act of Faith

Rest requires faith because it requires relinquishing control. It acknowledges limitation and dependence on God. Many people struggle with rest because they believe outcomes depend entirely on their effort.

Scripture teaches otherwise.

God works through obedience, not exhaustion. He multiplies faithfulness, not overextension. Rest does not remove responsibility; it restores capacity to fulfill it.

Choosing rest is often an act of obedience rather than convenience. It requires trusting God with unfinished tasks, unanswered emails, unmet expectations, and delayed progress.

God honors trust expressed through rest.

Understanding Recovery Beyond Sleep

Sleep is essential, but recovery involves more than sleep alone. Recovery restores physical, mental, emotional, and spiritual capacity. Without holistic recovery, sleep alone cannot compensate for chronic depletion.

Recovery includes:
slowing down mentally
releasing emotional tension
reducing constant stimulation
creating margin in schedules
allowing the nervous system to calm

Many people sleep but never truly rest. Their bodies stop moving, but their minds continue racing. Recovery requires intentional disengagement from constant input.

God designed rest to be restorative, not merely passive.

The Nervous System and Rest

The nervous system plays a critical role in recovery. Chronic stress keeps the body in a state of alertness. Even when danger is absent, the body remains braced. This constant readiness drains energy and weakens resilience.

Rest allows the nervous system to reset. It signals safety. It reduces stress hormones. It restores balance.

Many people cannot rest effectively because they have lived too long in survival mode. Their bodies have forgotten how to relax. Recovery in these cases is gradual and requires patience.

God meets people gently in this process.

Rest and Emotional Regulation

Physical rest supports emotional stability. Exhaustion amplifies emotion. Minor frustrations feel overwhelming. Small disappointments feel devastating. Patience shortens. Compassion fades.

Many emotional struggles lessen when rest improves. This does not replace emotional healing, but it supports it. A rested body provides a stable foundation for emotional resilience.

God designed rest to protect emotional capacity.

Boundaries That Protect Rest

Rest requires boundaries. Without boundaries, rest is constantly interrupted or postponed. Many people struggle to rest because they have not learned to protect it.

Boundaries around time, availability, and expectations preserve recovery. Saying no, delaying response, and limiting access are not acts of selfishness — they are acts of stewardship.

Jesus demonstrated boundaries without guilt. He did not explain every decision. He did not meet every demand. His boundaries allowed Him to remain effective.

An aligned life honors rest by protecting it.

Rest During Busy Seasons

Busy seasons test commitment to rest. Responsibilities increase. Time compresses. Energy drains faster. These seasons tempt people to abandon rest entirely.

God does not require perfect rest during demanding seasons. He requires **intentional rest**.

Rest during busy seasons may look smaller — shorter pauses, earlier sleep, simplified routines, reduced expectations. These adjustments preserve capacity without requiring unrealistic change.

Ignoring rest during busy seasons accelerates burnout. Honoring rest sustains endurance.

Recovery Is Not Linear

Recovery does not follow a straight line. Some days feel restorative. Others feel restless. Progress may feel uneven. This is normal.

God values consistency over perfection. Recovery deepens gradually as rhythms stabilize. Patience is essential. Forcing rest defeats its purpose.

God restores gently.

The Relationship Between Rest and Joy

Joy often returns through rest.

Exhaustion dulls joy. Creativity fades. Gratitude weakens. When rest is restored, joy often resurfaces naturally. Laughter feels easier. Perspective improves. Hope strengthens.

God desires joy for His people, not constant strain. Rest creates space for joy to breathe.

Rest and Longevity

Purpose is long-term. Calling unfolds over years, not weeks. Longevity requires sustainable rhythms. Rest protects longevity by preserving strength, health, and clarity.

Many people burn out not because their calling is too heavy, but because their rhythms are misaligned. God designed rest to protect purpose from destruction.

Living a Restored Life

Living restored does not mean life becomes slow or easy. It means life becomes balanced. Effort and recovery coexist. Work and rest support each other.

When rest is honored:
energy stabilizes
clarity improves
emotions regulate
endurance strengthens

The body becomes capable of carrying purpose without resentment.

God does not glorify exhaustion.
He honors obedience expressed through rest.

To live **Aligned for Purpose**, physical rest and recovery must be embraced as essential stewardship. They protect the body, sustain the mind, support the heart, and preserve the strength required to fulfill God's calling over time.

Scriptures Referenced in This Chapter

- Genesis 2:2–3
- Psalm 127:2
- Matthew 11:28–30
- Mark 6:31
- Exodus 33:14
- Isaiah 30:15

Chapter 13 — Mental Clarity and Focus: Quieting the Noise That Dilutes Purpose

Clarity is not the absence of responsibility.
It is the presence of direction.

Many people live mentally overwhelmed not because life is meaningless, but because life is noisy. Demands multiply. Information never stops. Expectations compete. The mind becomes crowded with decisions, reminders, worries, and unfinished thoughts. Even people who are disciplined, faithful, and hardworking often feel scattered rather than focused.

God never intended the mind to function as a constant holding space for everything.

Mental clarity is not about doing less. It is about seeing clearly enough to do what matters most without distraction, confusion, or exhaustion. When clarity is missing, purpose feels diluted. Effort increases, but impact decreases. Focus weakens, and energy is consumed by mental clutter rather than directed intention.

An aligned life requires mental clarity because purpose cannot be sustained where attention is constantly fragmented.

Why the Mind Becomes Noisy

The modern mind is overstimulated. It processes far more input than it was designed to carry. Notifications, conversations, responsibilities, memories, expectations, and future planning all compete for attention simultaneously.

Over time, the mind adapts by multitasking constantly. This adaptation feels productive, but it actually fractures focus. Mental energy is divided rather than directed. The result is fatigue without fulfillment.

Noise does not always come from chaos.
Often, it comes from **too many good things competing at once.**

God's design for the mind includes focus, not overload.

Mental Clutter and Its Hidden Cost

Mental clutter consists of unresolved thoughts, postponed decisions, lingering worries, and unprocessed information. Each unresolved item occupies mental space. Over time, this clutter accumulates and creates a sense of heaviness that is difficult to explain.

Mental clutter produces:
constant distraction
difficulty concentrating
emotional irritability
decision fatigue
restlessness

Many people attempt to address these symptoms through productivity tools alone. While tools can help, clarity ultimately requires **mental alignment**, not just organization.

God addresses the root, not only the symptoms.

Focus as a Spiritual Discipline

Focus is not merely a mental skill — it is a spiritual discipline. Scripture repeatedly emphasizes singleness of purpose, clarity of direction, and intentional attention. A scattered mind struggles to hear God clearly, not because God is silent, but because attention is divided.

Focus requires choosing where attention goes rather than allowing it to be pulled everywhere. This choice must be made repeatedly, because distraction is persistent.

A focused life is not rigid.
It is intentional.

God honors focused obedience more than scattered effort.

The Myth of Multitasking

Multitasking is often praised as efficiency. In reality, it fragments attention and reduces effectiveness. The mind does not truly multitask — it switches rapidly between tasks, losing focus each time.

This constant switching drains mental energy. It increases errors, reduces creativity, and weakens memory. Over time, multitasking becomes mental exhaustion disguised as productivity.

God's design favors presence over fragmentation. Presence allows clarity to deepen and focus to strengthen.

Decision Fatigue and Mental Exhaustion

Every decision consumes mental energy. When the mind is required to make constant decisions without recovery, fatigue sets in. Decision fatigue leads to impulsive choices, avoidance, or mental shutdown.

Many people experience decision fatigue daily without recognizing it. They feel mentally tired but cannot identify why. Clarity diminishes not because ability is lacking, but because energy has been depleted.

Mental clarity improves when decisions are simplified, prioritized, and aligned with purpose.

God's wisdom often brings simplicity rather than complexity.

Learning to Quiet the Mind

Quieting the mind does not mean silencing thoughts completely. It means reducing unnecessary noise so important thoughts can surface.

This requires intentional pauses — moments where the mind is allowed to settle rather than remain stimulated. Silence creates space for reflection. Stillness allows clarity to emerge.

Scripture consistently connects stillness with understanding. Quieting the mind is not avoidance; it is preparation.

God speaks most clearly where attention is available.

Mental Boundaries That Protect Focus

Just as physical boundaries protect rest, mental boundaries protect clarity. Without them, the mind remains open to constant intrusion.

Mental boundaries include:
limiting unnecessary input
protecting focused time
reducing exposure to constant noise
setting expectations around availability

These boundaries are not restrictive — they are protective. They preserve mental capacity for what truly matters.

Jesus modeled mental boundaries. He withdrew from crowds. He disengaged from constant demand. He focused on assignment rather than applause.

An aligned life honors mental boundaries without guilt.

Clarity Through Prioritization

Mental clarity increases when priorities are clear. When everything feels important, nothing receives proper attention. Prioritization is not neglect; it is wisdom.

God's guidance often clarifies what matters most rather than overwhelming with everything at once. Prioritization reduces anxiety by narrowing focus.

When priorities are aligned with purpose, decisions become easier. Mental energy is preserved rather than scattered.

Focus and Emotional Regulation

Mental clarity supports emotional stability. When the mind is cluttered, emotions intensify. Small frustrations feel overwhelming. Focused thinking calms emotional response.

Clarity creates perspective. Perspective reduces emotional volatility. A clear mind responds rather than reacts.

God designed clarity to protect emotional health.

The Role of Rest in Mental Focus

Mental focus requires rest. A fatigued mind cannot sustain attention. Rest restores clarity by allowing the brain to reset.

Many people attempt to improve focus without improving rest. This approach is ineffective. Mental clarity is supported by physical recovery.

God designed rest to sharpen focus, not diminish it.

Clarity During Overwhelming Seasons

Some seasons are inherently overwhelming. Responsibilities increase. Time compresses. Demands multiply. Mental clarity during these seasons looks different.

Clarity does not mean everything feels calm. It means direction remains steady. Focus narrows to what is necessary. Nonessential tasks are released without guilt.

God provides clarity suited to season, not perfection.

Training the Mind for Focus

Focus improves with practice. Each time attention is redirected intentionally, mental discipline strengthens. This process is gradual and requires patience.

The mind resists change at first. Over time, clarity becomes more natural as patterns shift.

God honors effort toward alignment, even when progress feels slow.

Mental Clarity Supports Purpose

Purpose requires attention. When focus is fragmented, purpose feels diluted. When clarity increases, purpose sharpens.

A clear mind:
recognizes direction

resists distraction
sustains effort
protects peace

Mental clarity does not eliminate difficulty — it prevents confusion from compounding it.

Living With Clear Focus

Living with mental clarity means engaging life with intention rather than reaction. It means choosing where attention goes rather than allowing constant intrusion.

When clarity is present:
decisions simplify
energy stabilizes
peace increases
purpose strengthens

God does not desire His people mentally overwhelmed and distracted. He desires clarity that allows purpose to be lived fully.

To live **Aligned for Purpose**, mental clarity and focus must be cultivated intentionally. Quieting the noise allows direction to emerge and purpose to remain steady.

Scriptures Referenced in This Chapter

- Proverbs 4:25–27
- Psalm 46:10
- James 1:5
- Isaiah 26:3
- Matthew 6:22–23
- Philippians 3:13–14

Chapter 14

Decision-Making With Wisdom: Choosing Alignment Over Impulse

Life is shaped less by intentions than by decisions.

Most people do not drift away from purpose suddenly. They drift gradually, one small decision at a time. These decisions are rarely dramatic or obvious. They are made in moments of pressure, fatigue, fear, or urgency. They feel reasonable in the moment, yet over time they compound into misalignment.

God never designed decision-making to be impulsive or reactive. He designed it to be **wise**.

Wisdom is not the absence of uncertainty. It is the ability to choose alignment even when outcomes are unclear. An aligned life is not built by perfect decisions, but by consistently choosing wisdom over impulse.

Purpose unfolds through decisions made faithfully over time.

Why Decisions Feel So Heavy

Decisions feel heavy because they carry consequence. Even small choices influence direction. The mind senses this weight, which often creates anxiety or avoidance. People either overthink decisions until paralysis sets in or rush decisions to escape discomfort.

Neither approach reflects God's design.

God does not demand certainty before obedience. He offers wisdom for each step. Decision-making becomes overwhelming when people believe they must see the entire path before taking the next step. Scripture teaches a different pattern — one of daily guidance.

Wisdom meets people in motion, not perfection.

Impulse Versus Alignment

Impulse reacts to emotion, urgency, or fear. Alignment responds to conviction, clarity, and trust. Impulsive decisions often feel relieving in the moment because they resolve tension quickly. Unfortunately, they frequently create new problems later.

Alignment slows the process.

Aligned decisions consider more than immediate relief. They account for long-term impact, spiritual peace, emotional stability, physical capacity, and financial responsibility. Alignment does not rush clarity; it waits for it.

God's guidance rarely pressures.
Pressure often comes from fear, not faith.

The Role of Emotion in Decision-Making

Emotions play a role in decision-making, but they were never meant to lead it. When emotions dominate decisions, consistency disappears. Choices fluctuate based on mood, stress, or exhaustion.

Wisdom listens to emotion without surrendering authority to it.

Fear urges escape.
Anger urges reaction.
Anxiety urges control.

God's wisdom invites pause. It creates space for discernment. Emotional awareness strengthens decision-making when it informs wisdom rather than overrides it.

An aligned life honors emotion without being ruled by it.

Decision Fatigue and Spiritual Drift

Decision fatigue weakens wisdom. When the mind is overloaded, people default to the easiest option, not the wisest. This is why fatigue is dangerous to alignment. Exhaustion lowers discernment.

Many poor decisions are made not out of rebellion, but out of weariness.

God understands human limitation. Scripture repeatedly emphasizes rest because rest restores judgment. When rest is ignored, decision quality declines.

Wise living protects energy so wisdom remains accessible.

The Quiet Voice of Conviction

God's guidance is often quieter than impulse. Conviction does not shout. It nudges. It settles. It brings peace even when the decision is difficult.

Many people miss conviction because they are listening for urgency. They assume God's direction will feel dramatic or obvious. Often, it feels calm, steady, and persistent.

Conviction remains consistent over time.
Impulse fades quickly.

An aligned life learns to recognize the difference.

Waiting as a Wise Decision

Waiting is a decision.

In a culture that values speed, waiting is often viewed as weakness. Scripture presents waiting as wisdom. Waiting allows clarity to develop, motives to surface, and peace to settle.

Some decisions are clarified not by action, but by patience. Waiting exposes whether urgency is driven by fear or faith. When waiting increases peace, it is often wisdom.

God does not rush people into decisions that will shape their future.

Counsel and Confirmation

Wisdom often comes through counsel. God places people in community because perspective sharpens discernment. Seeking wise counsel is not insecurity — it is humility.

However, counsel must be discerning. Not every opinion is wise. Godly counsel aligns with Scripture, peace, and purpose rather than personal agenda.

Confirmation does not always come through signs. Often, it comes through consistent peace, repeated conviction, and alignment across multiple areas of life.

God confirms direction through clarity, not confusion.

Alignment Across the Five Pillars

Wise decisions consider alignment across all pillars — spiritual, mental, emotional, physical, and financial.

A decision may feel spiritually exciting but emotionally draining.
It may be financially promising but physically unsustainable.
It may be mentally stimulating but spiritually distracting.

Wisdom evaluates the whole picture. Alignment does not sacrifice one pillar to elevate another. When a decision weakens multiple areas of life, it deserves reconsideration.

God's design is holistic.
Wisdom protects wholeness.

Fear-Based Decisions and Their Cost

Fear produces urgency. It pushes people to decide quickly to regain control. Fear-based decisions often feel necessary in the moment, but they compromise peace.

Fear says:
"If you don't act now, you'll miss it."
"If you don't say yes, you'll lose it."
"If you wait, everything will fall apart."

Wisdom asks:
"Does this align?"
"Does this produce peace?"
"Does this honor my capacity and calling?"

God does not lead through fear.
Fear distorts discernment.

Learning From Past Decisions Without Shame

Past decisions often carry regret. Many people avoid reflection because it triggers shame. God invites reflection for learning, not condemnation.

Wisdom grows through experience. Reviewing past decisions reveals patterns — where impulse led, where patience protected, where fear misled, and where trust sustained.

Shame immobilizes.
Learning empowers.

God redeems even misaligned decisions by producing wisdom through them.

The Courage to Say No

Some of the wisest decisions are refusals. Saying no requires courage, especially when opportunity, approval, or pressure is involved.

Wisdom understands that saying yes to everything dilutes purpose. Every yes carries responsibility. Saying no protects focus, energy, and alignment.

Jesus said no regularly. He declined demands, resisted pressure, and stayed focused on assignment. His refusals preserved His effectiveness.

An aligned life honors no as a holy boundary.

Decision-Making in Uncertain Seasons

Some seasons lack clarity. Direction feels blurred. Progress slows. In these seasons, wisdom focuses on faithfulness rather than foresight.

When clarity is absent:
Do what is right.
Remain consistent.
Avoid impulsive change.
Protect peace.

God often withholds clarity not to frustrate, but to deepen trust. Faithfulness in uncertainty strengthens discernment for future decisions.

Consistency Builds Confidence

Confidence in decision-making grows through consistency. Each aligned decision reinforces trust in discernment. Over time, fear loosens its grip. Decisions feel less overwhelming.

Wisdom is built, not inherited.

God develops discernment gradually as people choose alignment repeatedly.

Living as a Wise Decision-Maker

Living wisely does not mean never making mistakes. It means learning to choose alignment over impulse, peace over pressure, and trust over fear.

When wisdom guides decisions:
clarity increases
regret decreases
peace strengthens
purpose stabilizes

God desires His people to live intentionally, not reactively.

To live **Aligned for Purpose**, decision-making must be guided by wisdom that honors God's design for wholeness. Each wise choice strengthens alignment and prepares the way for purpose to unfold with peace.

Scriptures Referenced in This Chapter

- Proverbs 3:5–6
- James 1:5
- Proverbs 19:20–21
- Isaiah 30:21
- Colossians 3:15
- Psalm 37:5

Chapter 15

Purpose in the Waiting: Faithfulness When Progress Feels Slow

Waiting is one of the most misunderstood seasons of life.

Many people believe waiting is wasted time — a pause between meaningful moments, an obstacle delaying progress, or evidence that something has gone wrong. In reality, waiting is often where the deepest formation occurs. It is where motives are purified, character is strengthened, and alignment is refined.

God never wastes waiting.

Purpose is not only revealed in movement. It is developed in stillness. Some of the most critical work God does happens when nothing appears to be happening at all. Waiting exposes impatience, fear, and control. It also builds trust, endurance, and maturity.

An aligned life learns how to remain faithful when progress feels slow.

Why Waiting Feels So Difficult

Waiting feels difficult because it removes control. It forces dependence. It slows momentum. In a culture that celebrates speed and results, waiting feels like failure. People begin to question themselves, their decisions, and even God.

Thoughts arise:
"Did I miss something?"
"Did I do something wrong?"
"Why is everyone else moving forward?"

These questions are natural, but they are not always rooted in truth. Scripture shows waiting as a normal part of purpose, not a detour from it.

God often delays outcomes not to withhold blessing, but to prepare capacity.

Waiting Exposes What Movement Hides

Constant movement can hide misalignment. Waiting reveals it.

When life slows, unresolved emotions surface. Insecurities emerge. Motives are tested. Without distraction, people are confronted with what they have avoided. This exposure is uncomfortable, but it is necessary.

Waiting strips away false confidence and replaces it with humility. It reveals whether faith is rooted in trust or results. God uses waiting to strengthen foundation so purpose does not collapse under future weight.

Growth that happens in waiting lasts longer than progress rushed through impatience.

The Difference Between Delay and Denial

One of the most damaging misunderstandings in faith is confusing delay with denial. Delay feels like rejection when expectation is high. Over time, discouragement sets in, and hope weakens.

Scripture repeatedly distinguishes between the two. God delays to align timing, develop readiness, and refine obedience. Denial redirects. Delay prepares.

When people misinterpret delay as denial, they often abandon purpose prematurely. They settle for substitutes, force outcomes, or disengage entirely.

God's timing is intentional, even when it is uncomfortable.

Waiting Refines Motive

Waiting reveals why something is desired.

Is it for affirmation?
For control?
For escape?
For security?

Or is it aligned with purpose?

When progress slows, motives are tested. God uses waiting to purify desire so that when fulfillment comes, it does not become an idol. What is received too quickly is often misused. What is waited for is stewarded with care.

Waiting strengthens alignment by aligning desire with wisdom.

Faithfulness Without Visibility

Waiting often lacks visibility. Progress is internal rather than external. This makes faithfulness feel unrewarded. Many people grow discouraged because they equate faithfulness with visible results.

Scripture teaches otherwise.

Faithfulness is obedience in obscurity. It is consistency without applause. It is trust without confirmation. God sees what others do not. He honors what is hidden.

Waiting trains people to live for God's approval rather than external validation.

Patience as Strength, Not Weakness

Patience is often mistaken for passivity. In truth, patience requires strength. It resists impulsive action. It endures discomfort. It trusts process.

Patience does not mean inactivity. It means remaining aligned while awaiting clarity. It involves preparation, growth, and obedience without rushing outcome.

God values patience because it produces maturity.

Waiting Protects Future Purpose

Many callings fail not because they were wrong, but because they were entered too early. Waiting protects purpose by ensuring readiness.

Responsibility received before capacity becomes a burden. Opportunity entered without preparation becomes pressure. Waiting develops endurance, humility, and discernment so purpose can be carried sustainably.

God cares more about longevity than immediacy.

What to Do While Waiting

Waiting is active, not idle.

It is a season for strengthening disciplines, refining character, deepening faith, and addressing areas of misalignment. Waiting invites reflection and growth rather than frustration.

Productive waiting involves:
remaining obedient in what is known
continuing to serve faithfully
protecting peace
avoiding comparison
trusting timing

God does not ask people to wait passively. He asks them to wait faithfully.

Resisting the Urge to Force Outcomes

Forcing outcomes creates misalignment. When people attempt to accelerate timing, they often compromise values, boundaries, or peace. What begins as impatience ends as regret.

God does not need help fulfilling His promises. Forced outcomes often produce unnecessary hardship.

Waiting builds trust. Forcing builds anxiety.

Waiting and Comparison

Comparison intensifies waiting. Watching others progress creates pressure to move prematurely. Comparison distorts perception and fuels discouragement.

God's timeline is personal. Comparing seasons creates frustration. Purpose unfolds uniquely for each person.

Waiting becomes lighter when comparison is released.

Learning to Trust God's Pace

Trusting God's pace requires surrender. It acknowledges that God sees the full picture while people see fragments. Trust develops as waiting deepens.

God's pace is not slow.
It is precise.

Every season has a purpose. Waiting seasons build foundations that visible seasons rely on.

Hope Sustained in Waiting

Waiting without hope becomes despair. Scripture encourages hope anchored in God's faithfulness rather than circumstances. Hope sustains endurance.

Hope does not deny difficulty.
It refuses to surrender to it.

God renews strength in those who wait with trust.

Waiting Ends, But Formation Remains

Waiting seasons eventually pass. Movement returns. Opportunity arrives. When it does, the formation gained through waiting remains.

Those who wait well move forward with confidence rather than insecurity. They carry purpose with humility rather than urgency. Waiting equips them to receive without fear.

God rewards faithfulness in waiting with readiness in fulfillment.

Living Aligned While Waiting

Living aligned while waiting means resisting pressure to rush, maintaining obedience without clarity, and trusting God's timing over personal preference.

When waiting is embraced:
character deepens
trust strengthens
discernment sharpens
peace stabilizes

God does not waste waiting.
He uses it to prepare people for purpose.

To live **Aligned for Purpose**, waiting must be understood not as delay, but as divine preparation. Faithfulness in waiting ensures purpose unfolds with strength, wisdom, and peace.

Scriptures Referenced in This Chapter

- Isaiah 40:31
- Psalm 27:14
- Habakkuk 2:3
- James 5:7–8
- Lamentations 3:25–26
- Galatians 6:9

Chapter 16

When Faith Becomes a Way of Life: Living Aligned Every Day

Faith was never meant to be occasional.

It was never designed to appear only in moments of crisis, worship, or reflection. Faith, in God's design, is meant to shape how life is lived daily — how decisions are made, how relationships are handled, how responsibilities are carried, and how challenges are endured. When faith remains compartmentalized, life feels divided. When faith becomes integrated, life gains coherence.

Many people believe in God deeply yet struggle to live with consistency. They pray sincerely but react impulsively. They trust God spiritually but operate anxiously in practical matters. They feel faithful on Sundays and fractured by Wednesdays. This disconnect does not mean faith is weak — it means faith has not yet been fully woven into daily life.

An aligned life is one where faith becomes **the operating system**, not an accessory.

Why Faith Often Feels Inconsistent

Faith feels inconsistent when it is treated as an activity rather than a posture. Activities happen at specific times. Postures shape everything.

When faith is reduced to moments — prayer time, church attendance, devotional reading — it competes with the rest of life instead of guiding it. The result is spiritual sincerity paired with practical inconsistency. People trust God in principle but default to fear, control, or impulse under pressure.

God never intended faith to be activated only when remembered. He intended it to be lived continuously.

Faith matures when it moves from belief to behavior, from intention to habit, from conviction to rhythm.

Faith Expressed Through Daily Choices

Faith becomes real when it shapes ordinary decisions.

It influences how a person responds to stress, how they speak when frustrated, how they handle money when anxious, how they treat others when tired, and how they rest when tempted to overwork. These moments rarely feel spiritual, yet they are the clearest expressions of faith.

Faith in daily life looks like:
choosing patience over reaction
choosing integrity over convenience
choosing rest over burnout
choosing trust over control

These choices are small, but they compound. Over time, they form a life that reflects alignment rather than contradiction.

God values daily obedience more than dramatic declarations.

Consistency Over Intensity

Many people pursue faith with intensity but lack consistency. They experience spiritual highs followed by exhaustion and disappointment. Intensity without consistency leads to burnout.

God's design favors steady faithfulness over emotional peaks. Consistency builds endurance. It stabilizes identity. It sustains alignment when motivation fades.

Faith lived daily does not require constant inspiration. It requires commitment. Commitment carries faith through seasons where feelings fluctuate and circumstances challenge belief.

An aligned life is built through repeated, faithful choices — not emotional momentum.

Faith in Pressure and Responsibility

Pressure reveals whether faith is practiced or professed.

When responsibility increases, faith is tested. Deadlines approach. Needs multiply. Expectations rise. In these moments, people often revert to control, anxiety, or overextension.

Living aligned means allowing faith to guide response under pressure rather than abandoning it for survival tactics. This does not remove responsibility — it changes how responsibility is carried.

Faith under pressure chooses:
calm over panic
wisdom over urgency
obedience over fear

God does not remove pressure from life. He provides stability within it.

Faith and Emotional Regulation

Faith lived daily supports emotional regulation. It does not suppress emotion — it steadies it. When faith is integrated, emotions are processed rather than avoided, expressed rather than exploded.

Faith reminds the heart of truth when emotion distorts perspective. It anchors response in trust rather than impulse. Over time, emotional reactions soften as faith becomes instinctive.

God designed faith to calm the soul, not complicate it.

Faith and the Body

Daily faith includes physical stewardship. Faith that ignores the body becomes impractical. God does not expect people to trust Him spiritually while neglecting themselves physically.

Living aligned means honoring rest, discipline, and recovery as acts of faith. It means recognizing limits without guilt and caring for the body as a vessel for purpose.

Faith that lives daily respects sustainability.

Faith and Work

Work is one of the primary places faith is expressed.

Integrity, diligence, humility, boundaries, and excellence all reflect faith in action. Work reveals values. It exposes whether faith guides behavior or remains theoretical.

Living aligned means allowing faith to shape work ethic without allowing work to replace faith. It balances responsibility with rest, ambition with contentment, effort with trust.

God honors work done faithfully, not obsessively.

Faith and Money

Faith lived daily shapes financial behavior. It influences spending, saving, giving, and planning. It resists fear-based decisions and promotes stewardship rooted in trust.

Financial faith is not reckless. It is wise. It acknowledges responsibility while trusting God as provider. It plans without panic and gives without pressure.

When faith guides finances, peace increases.

Faith in Relationships

Relationships reveal whether faith has become a way of life. Patience, forgiveness, boundaries, humility, and honesty are all expressions of faith lived relationally.

Living aligned means responding to conflict with wisdom rather than ego, addressing issues rather than avoiding them, and loving without losing identity.

Faith that remains private but fails relationally is incomplete.

Faith Without Performance

One of the greatest obstacles to daily faith is performance mentality. Many people believe faith must look impressive to be valid. This belief creates pressure and inconsistency.

God does not require performance. He desires presence.

Faith lived daily is quiet, steady, and sincere. It does not seek attention. It seeks alignment. It is visible through character rather than display.

God values authenticity over appearance.

Faith Through Ordinary Faithfulness

Most of life is ordinary. It consists of routine, responsibility, repetition, and quiet perseverance. Faith that only functions in extraordinary moments will feel absent most of the time.

Living aligned means honoring God in the ordinary. It means trusting Him in routine, obeying Him in repetition, and serving Him without recognition.

God often does His deepest work in ordinary faithfulness.

When Faith Feels Weak

There will be seasons when faith feels weak. Doubt arises. Weariness sets in. Confidence fades. Living aligned does not mean faith never wavers — it means faith is returned to God rather than abandoned.

God is not threatened by weakness. He meets people in it. Faith that is brought honestly to God grows stronger through humility.

Weak faith surrendered is stronger than confident faith concealed.

A Life That Reflects Alignment

When faith becomes a way of life, alignment becomes visible.

Decisions reflect wisdom.
Relationships reflect maturity.
Work reflects integrity.

Rest reflects trust.
Purpose reflects peace.

Life feels less divided. Faith no longer competes with reality — it governs it.

This is the life God designed.

Living Aligned for the Long Term

Faith lived daily sustains purpose over the long term. It protects against burnout, inconsistency, and fragmentation. It allows life to be lived with intention rather than reaction.

God did not design faith to be carried occasionally.
He designed it to be lived fully.

To live **Aligned for Purpose**, faith must move beyond moments and become a way of life — steady, integrated, and faithful in every season.

Scriptures Referenced in This Chapter

- Proverbs 3:5–6
- Galatians 2:20
- Colossians 3:17
- James 2:17
- Micah 6:8
- Romans 12:1–2

Chapter 16

When Faith Becomes a Way of Life: Living Aligned Every Day

Faith was never meant to be occasional.

It was never designed to appear only in moments of crisis, worship, or reflection. Faith, in God's design, is meant to shape how life is lived daily — how decisions are made, how relationships are handled, how responsibilities are carried, and how challenges are endured. When faith remains compartmentalized, life feels divided. When faith becomes integrated, life gains coherence.

Many people believe in God deeply yet struggle to live with consistency. They pray sincerely but react impulsively. They trust God spiritually but operate anxiously in practical matters. They feel faithful on Sundays and fractured by Wednesdays. This disconnect does not mean faith is weak — it means faith has not yet been fully woven into daily life.

An aligned life is one where faith becomes **the operating system**, not an accessory.

Why Faith Often Feels Inconsistent

Faith feels inconsistent when it is treated as an activity rather than a posture. Activities happen at specific times. Postures shape everything.

When faith is reduced to moments — prayer time, church attendance, devotional reading — it competes with the rest of life instead of guiding it. The result is spiritual sincerity paired with practical inconsistency. People trust God in principle but default to fear, control, or impulse under pressure.

God never intended faith to be activated only when remembered. He intended it to be lived continuously.

Faith matures when it moves from belief to behavior, from intention to habit, from conviction to rhythm.

Faith Expressed Through Daily Choices

Faith becomes real when it shapes ordinary decisions.

It influences how a person responds to stress, how they speak when frustrated, how they handle money when anxious, how they treat others when tired, and how they rest when tempted to overwork. These moments rarely feel spiritual, yet they are the clearest expressions of faith.

Faith in daily life looks like:
choosing patience over reaction
choosing integrity over convenience
choosing rest over burnout
choosing trust over control

These choices are small, but they compound. Over time, they form a life that reflects alignment rather than contradiction.

God values daily obedience more than dramatic declarations.

Consistency Over Intensity

Many people pursue faith with intensity but lack consistency. They experience spiritual highs followed by exhaustion and disappointment. Intensity without consistency leads to burnout.

God's design favors steady faithfulness over emotional peaks. Consistency builds endurance. It stabilizes identity. It sustains alignment when motivation fades.

Faith lived daily does not require constant inspiration. It requires commitment. Commitment carries faith through seasons where feelings fluctuate and circumstances challenge belief.

An aligned life is built through repeated, faithful choices — not emotional momentum.

Faith in Pressure and Responsibility

Pressure reveals whether faith is practiced or professed.

When responsibility increases, faith is tested. Deadlines approach. Needs multiply. Expectations rise. In these moments, people often revert to control, anxiety, or overextension.

Living aligned means allowing faith to guide response under pressure rather than abandoning it for survival tactics. This does not remove responsibility — it changes how responsibility is carried.

Faith under pressure chooses:
calm over panic
wisdom over urgency
obedience over fear

God does not remove pressure from life. He provides stability within it.

Faith and Emotional Regulation

Faith lived daily supports emotional regulation. It does not suppress emotion — it steadies it. When faith is integrated, emotions are processed rather than avoided, expressed rather than exploded.

Faith reminds the heart of truth when emotion distorts perspective. It anchors response in trust rather than impulse. Over time, emotional reactions soften as faith becomes instinctive.

God designed faith to calm the soul, not complicate it.

Faith and the Body

Daily faith includes physical stewardship. Faith that ignores the body becomes impractical. God does not expect people to trust Him spiritually while neglecting themselves physically.

Living aligned means honoring rest, discipline, and recovery as acts of faith. It means recognizing limits without guilt and caring for the body as a vessel for purpose.

Faith that lives daily respects sustainability.

Faith and Work

Work is one of the primary places faith is expressed.

Integrity, diligence, humility, boundaries, and excellence all reflect faith in action. Work reveals values. It exposes whether faith guides behavior or remains theoretical.

Living aligned means allowing faith to shape work ethic without allowing work to replace faith. It balances responsibility with rest, ambition with contentment, effort with trust.

God honors work done faithfully, not obsessively.

Faith and Money

Faith lived daily shapes financial behavior. It influences spending, saving, giving, and planning. It resists fear-based decisions and promotes stewardship rooted in trust.

Financial faith is not reckless. It is wise. It acknowledges responsibility while trusting God as provider. It plans without panic and gives without pressure.

When faith guides finances, peace increases.

Faith in Relationships

Relationships reveal whether faith has become a way of life. Patience, forgiveness, boundaries, humility, and honesty are all expressions of faith lived relationally.

Living aligned means responding to conflict with wisdom rather than ego, addressing issues rather than avoiding them, and loving without losing identity.

Faith that remains private but fails relationally is incomplete.

Faith Without Performance

One of the greatest obstacles to daily faith is performance mentality. Many people believe faith must look impressive to be valid. This belief creates pressure and inconsistency.

God does not require performance. He desires presence.

Faith lived daily is quiet, steady, and sincere. It does not seek attention. It seeks alignment. It is visible through character rather than display.

God values authenticity over appearance.

Faith Through Ordinary Faithfulness

Most of life is ordinary. It consists of routine, responsibility, repetition, and quiet perseverance. Faith that only functions in extraordinary moments will feel absent most of the time.

Living aligned means honoring God in the ordinary. It means trusting Him in routine, obeying Him in repetition, and serving Him without recognition.

God often does His deepest work in ordinary faithfulness.

When Faith Feels Weak

There will be seasons when faith feels weak. Doubt arises. Weariness sets in. Confidence fades. Living aligned does not mean faith never wavers — it means faith is returned to God rather than abandoned.

God is not threatened by weakness. He meets people in it. Faith that is brought honestly to God grows stronger through humility.

Weak faith surrendered is stronger than confident faith concealed.

A Life That Reflects Alignment

When faith becomes a way of life, alignment becomes visible.

Decisions reflect wisdom.
Relationships reflect maturity.
Work reflects integrity.

Rest reflects trust.
Purpose reflects peace.

Life feels less divided. Faith no longer competes with reality — it governs it.

This is the life God designed.

Living Aligned for the Long Term

Faith lived daily sustains purpose over the long term. It protects against burnout, inconsistency, and fragmentation. It allows life to be lived with intention rather than reaction.

God did not design faith to be carried occasionally.
He designed it to be lived fully.

To live **Aligned for Purpose**, faith must move beyond moments and become a way of life — steady, integrated, and faithful in every season.

Scriptures Referenced in This Chapter

- Proverbs 3:5–6
- Galatians 2:20
- Colossians 3:17
- James 2:17
- Micah 6:8
- Romans 12:1–2

Chapter 17

Walking in Obedience: Choosing God's Way When It Costs You

Obedience is one of the most misunderstood and most powerful forces in a believer's life.

It is often reduced to rule-keeping, obligation, or restriction, when in reality obedience is alignment in motion. It is the choice to trust God's wisdom over personal preference, His timing over urgency, and His direction over convenience. Obedience is not about perfection; it is about posture. It reveals who — or what — is truly guiding a person's life.

God never intended obedience to be a burden.
He intended it to be protection.

An aligned life is not built on emotional enthusiasm or spiritual intensity alone. It is built on obedience practiced consistently, especially when it is uncomfortable, unseen, or costly. Obedience shapes character quietly and directs life steadily. Long before purpose becomes visible, obedience forms the foundation that can carry it.

Why Obedience Feels So Challenging

Obedience feels challenging because it confronts independence.

Human nature prefers control. It wants to understand outcomes before committing, to feel safe before surrendering, and to receive assurance before acting. Obedience often asks for the opposite. It requires movement without certainty, trust without evidence, and faith without immediate reward.

Many people struggle with obedience not because they lack faith, but because they fear loss — loss of comfort, approval, opportunity, or familiarity. Obedience often requires letting go of something that feels secure in order to follow something that feels uncertain.

Yet Scripture consistently shows that what obedience costs in comfort, it restores in clarity and peace.

Obedience Is Direction, Not Punishment

One of the most damaging misconceptions about obedience is the belief that God uses it to restrict joy or control behavior. This belief often comes from experiences with authority that was harsh, inconsistent, or conditional.

God's obedience is different.

Obedience is directional. It keeps life aligned with purpose. It prevents unnecessary detours, protects from self-inflicted wounds, and preserves peace. God does not demand obedience to limit life, but to guide it.

When obedience is ignored, confusion increases. When obedience is embraced, direction clarifies.

God's commands are not arbitrary. They are rooted in wisdom.

The Hidden Cost of Disobedience

Disobedience rarely feels dramatic in the moment. It often appears subtle, practical, or justified. People explain it away as necessity, timing, or self-preservation. Over time, however, disobedience accumulates cost.

It produces:
inner conflict
loss of peace
spiritual dullness
emotional strain
directional confusion

Disobedience does not remove faith — it weakens alignment. Life becomes harder not because God withdraws, but because wisdom has been bypassed.

God allows people to choose, but He does not remove consequences from misalignment.

Obedience and Identity

Obedience is deeply connected to identity.

When identity is fragile, obedience feels threatening. People fear that obedience will cost them approval, belonging, or worth. They hesitate to obey because they are unsure of who they are without external validation.

When identity is secure, obedience becomes an act of trust rather than fear.

God never asks obedience to strip identity. He uses obedience to refine it. Each obedient choice reinforces identity rooted in Him rather than circumstance.

Secure identity produces willing obedience.
Insecure identity resists it.

Delayed Obedience and Rationalization

Delayed obedience often disguises itself as wisdom.

People say they are waiting for clarity, better timing, or confirmation. While discernment matters, obedience that is endlessly postponed becomes avoidance. Rationalization replaces surrender.

Scripture consistently shows that God honors timely obedience. Delays born from fear or comfort weaken trust and prolong struggle.

God does not rush obedience, but He does not endorse indefinite hesitation.

Obedience Without Applause

One of the hardest realities of obedience is that it is often unseen.

Many obedient choices go unnoticed by others. There is no applause for integrity, restraint, forgiveness, or consistency. This invisibility tests motive. Obedience rooted in external validation will not last long.

God values obedience done in secret because it reveals sincerity. What is hidden is not wasted. God sees alignment even when others do not.

Faithfulness in obscurity prepares people for responsibility in visibility.

Obedience and Emotional Resistance

Obedience often encounters emotional resistance.

Fear questions safety.
Anger resents surrender.
Desire negotiates compromise.

These emotions are not signs that obedience is wrong. They are signals that growth is occurring. Emotional discomfort often accompanies transformation.

God does not require emotional agreement to obey. He invites obedience that leads emotions into alignment rather than waiting for emotions to lead.

Maturity develops when obedience is chosen despite emotional resistance.

Obedience in Relationships

Relationships test obedience profoundly.

God may call a person to forgive when resentment feels justified, to set boundaries when attachment feels strong, to speak truth when silence feels safer, or to step away when familiarity feels comforting.

Relational obedience often costs approval, comfort, or familiarity. Yet it protects emotional health and preserves peace.

God's instructions in relationships are rooted in wisdom, not avoidance. Obedience in relationships aligns love with truth.

Obedience Under Pressure

Pressure exposes whether obedience is practiced or merely preferred.

When stress increases, people default to habits. They rush, control, or compromise. Obedience under pressure requires intentional trust — choosing alignment even when urgency demands shortcuts.

God does not remove pressure to make obedience easier. He strengthens people to obey within pressure.

Obedience under pressure produces deep spiritual confidence.

Trusting God's Character

At its core, obedience is about trust.

People obey those they trust. When God is viewed as faithful, obedience feels reasonable. When God is viewed as unpredictable or harsh, obedience feels dangerous.

Many struggles with obedience stem from distorted views of God rather than defiance. Healing these views restores willingness.

God's character makes obedience safe.

Separation That Protects Alignment

Sometimes obedience creates separation.

It may distance a person from environments, relationships, or habits that no longer align with God's direction. This separation can feel lonely or confusing, but it is often protective.

God separates to preserve purpose, not to punish. What obedience removes is often replaced with healthier alignment later.

Loss experienced through obedience is rarely permanent.

Obedience Builds Spiritual Authority

Spiritual authority is not position — it is alignment.

Authority grows when life consistently reflects God's direction. Discernment sharpens. Confidence stabilizes. Peace becomes accessible. Obedience builds authority quietly through consistency.

God entrusts responsibility to those who obey faithfully, not flawlessly.

Daily Obedience Shapes Destiny

Obedience is rarely a single dramatic moment. It is a daily pattern.

It shows up in how time is stewarded, how words are chosen, how boundaries are honored, how integrity is protected. These choices seem small, but they compound powerfully.

Daily obedience shapes destiny more than occasional spiritual intensity.

The Fruit of Obedience

Obedience produces fruit over time:
clarity
peace
confidence
stability
endurance

The fruit may not appear immediately, but it is consistent. Obedience aligns life with God's design and reduces unnecessary struggle.

God does not withhold blessing.
He protects it through obedience.

Living an Obedient Life

Living obediently does not mean life becomes easy. It means life becomes aligned.

Challenges remain, but confusion decreases. Pressure exists, but peace remains accessible. Direction clarifies, and trust deepens.

God does not call obedience to control His people.
He invites obedience to guide them.

To live **Aligned for Purpose**, obedience must be embraced not as obligation, but as trust expressed through action. Each obedient choice strengthens alignment and prepares the way for purpose to unfold with wisdom, stability, and peace.

Scriptures Referenced in This Chapter

- 1 Samuel 15:22
- John 14:15
- Deuteronomy 30:19–20
- Luke 11:28
- James 1:22
- Proverbs 16:3

Chapter 18

Endurance and Perseverance: Staying Faithful When the Journey Is Long

Endurance is rarely celebrated, yet it is essential to purpose.

Most people admire beginnings and applaud breakthroughs. They celebrate the launch, the announcement, the visible success. What is rarely acknowledged is the long, quiet middle — the years of repetition, responsibility, delay, discipline, and unseen faithfulness. This is where endurance is formed.

Endurance is not excitement.
It is **staying**.

It is continuing when progress feels slow, when motivation fades, when results are unclear, and when obedience no longer feels heroic. God designed endurance as a necessary strength because purpose is not fulfilled quickly. It unfolds through seasons that test patience, faith, and resilience.

An aligned life requires endurance because calling without endurance collapses under time.

Why the Journey Feels Longer Than Expected

Many people begin their faith journey with the assumption that obedience will lead quickly to clarity, ease, or visible reward. When progress slows, disappointment sets in. They begin to question their direction, their calling, or even God.

Scripture shows a consistent pattern: purpose unfolds gradually.

God often reveals direction before readiness. He speaks promise long before fulfillment. This gap between promise and manifestation is not punishment — it is preparation.

The journey feels long because growth takes time. Character must be strengthened. Perspective must mature. Capacity must increase. God builds endurance so purpose can be carried without collapse.

The Difference Between Endurance and Survival

Endurance is not survival.

Survival is reactive. It is fueled by fear, urgency, and exhaustion. Survival does what is necessary to get through the moment. Endurance is intentional. It is sustained by trust, discipline, and hope.

Many people survive seasons they were meant to endure. They push through without processing, reflect without renewing, and persist without rest. Over time, survival drains joy and weakens faith.

God never intended His people to merely survive.
He designed them to endure with strength and peace.

Endurance includes rest, reflection, and renewal. It is steady rather than frantic. It honors rhythm rather than forcing momentum.

Endurance Develops Through Repetition

Endurance is built through repetition, not intensity.

Doing the right thing once does not build endurance. Doing the right thing consistently does. Showing up again after disappointment. Choosing obedience again after delay. Continuing faithfulness when recognition is absent.

Repetition forms resilience. It strengthens trust. It deepens discipline. Over time, repetition transforms effort into habit and habit into character.

God values faithfulness over flash. Endurance grows quietly through repeated alignment.

The Emotional Weight of Long Seasons

Long seasons carry emotional weight.

Hope rises and falls. Discouragement whispers. Fatigue accumulates. Many people feel guilty for growing weary, believing faith should eliminate exhaustion. Scripture tells a different story.

Even the most faithful grow tired.

Endurance does not deny weariness. It addresses it wisely. God invites honesty in fatigue, not denial. He renews strength, not shames weakness.

Weariness is not failure.
It is a signal to restore, not quit.

Perseverance Without Bitterness

One of the greatest dangers in long journeys is bitterness.

When progress is slow and sacrifices are many, resentment can form quietly. People begin to feel overlooked, unappreciated, or taken for granted. They continue outwardly, but inwardly they grow hardened.

Bitterness poisons endurance.

God does not ask people to persevere resentfully. He invites perseverance rooted in hope. Hope protects the heart from bitterness by keeping perspective anchored in purpose rather than circumstance.

Endurance sustained by hope remains soft, not hardened.

Endurance and Identity

Identity determines endurance.

When identity is tied to outcomes, endurance weakens during delay. When identity is rooted in God, endurance strengthens regardless of results. People who know who they are can continue even when affirmation is absent.

God forms identity before outcome so endurance does not collapse when progress stalls.

Endurance is easier when worth is not measured by visibility.

Perseverance Through Unanswered Questions

Many endurance seasons include unanswered questions.

Why is this taking so long?
Why did that opportunity close?
Why does progress feel uneven?

God does not always answer questions immediately. Sometimes He strengthens trust before providing clarity. Faithfulness in uncertainty deepens reliance on God rather than understanding.

Perseverance does not require full understanding.
It requires trust.

Endurance Requires Rhythm, Not Constant Effort

One of the most common mistakes in long journeys is confusing endurance with constant exertion. People push relentlessly, believing rest will slow progress. In reality, rest preserves endurance.

God designed endurance to include rhythm — effort and recovery, movement and stillness, sowing and waiting. Ignoring rhythm leads to burnout, not perseverance.

Endurance honors rest as a strength, not a weakness.

The Role of Hope in Perseverance

Hope fuels endurance.

Without hope, perseverance becomes obligation. With hope, perseverance becomes expectation. Hope does not deny difficulty; it anticipates faithfulness.

God renews hope by reminding people of His character, not by promising ease. Hope anchored in God's faithfulness sustains endurance through uncertainty.

Hope keeps the heart forward-facing even when progress feels slow.

Perseverance When Results Are Invisible

Some of the most important work happens invisibly.

Character forms. Faith deepens. Discernment sharpens. These developments are not measurable, yet they are essential. Many people abandon endurance because they cannot see progress.

God sees what is being built beneath the surface.

What is invisible now often supports what becomes visible later.

Learning to Stay Without Losing Joy

Endurance does not mean joyless persistence.

God desires endurance that is sustainable and life-giving. Joy often returns when perspective shifts from urgency to trust. Joy grows when endurance is shared with God rather than carried alone.

Endurance paired with joy strengthens faith rather than draining it.

The Reward of Endurance

Endurance is rewarded — not always with immediate success, but with depth, stability, and readiness.

Those who endure well:
carry peace under pressure
remain steady in transition
walk confidently in purpose
serve without resentment

God honors endurance because it reflects trust in His timing.

Endurance Prepares You for What Comes Next

Many people ask God to move them forward without realizing they are being strengthened for what lies ahead. Endurance seasons prepare people for increased responsibility, influence, and impact.

God does not delay purpose arbitrarily.
He prepares people intentionally.

Endurance ensures that when opportunity arrives, collapse does not follow.

Living an Enduring Life

Living with endurance means choosing faithfulness repeatedly, even when motivation fades. It means honoring rhythm, guarding the heart, and trusting God's pace.

Endurance is not glamorous.
It is powerful.

To live **Aligned for Purpose**, endurance and perseverance must be embraced as essential strengths. They sustain faith, protect peace, and ensure purpose unfolds with maturity rather than collapse.

Scriptures Referenced in This Chapter

- Hebrews 12:1–3
- James 1:2–4
- Galatians 6:9
- Isaiah 40:31
- Romans 5:3–5
- Psalm 66:10–12

Chapter 19

Financial Peace and Provision: Living Free From the Grip of Fear

Financial pressure has a way of shaping how people live, think, and even pray.

For many, money is not just a resource — it is a constant concern. It influences decisions, relationships, sleep, self-worth, and spiritual confidence. Even people who love God deeply can live under persistent financial anxiety, believing peace will come *after* provision arrives.

God's design is the opposite.

Financial peace is not the result of abundance.
It is the result of **alignment**.

An aligned life does not ignore financial responsibility, nor does it idolize financial security. It understands provision as partnership — God as the source, people as stewards. When this order is reversed, fear takes over. When it is restored, peace follows.

Purpose cannot thrive where financial fear dominates.

Why Money Creates So Much Anxiety

Money touches survival. It affects housing, food, safety, opportunity, and dignity. When finances feel unstable, the nervous system responds as though danger is present. This response is human, not sinful.

However, when fear becomes the primary guide, wisdom fades.

Financial anxiety often comes from:
past instability
unexpected loss
lack of education
comparison
responsibility overload

Over time, fear trains the mind to expect lack even when provision is present. People live reactively — hoarding, overspending, avoiding, or obsessing — rather than stewarding intentionally.

God never intended money to control emotions.
He intended it to serve life.

Provision Versus Control

One of the greatest struggles in financial alignment is the desire for control.

Control feels safer than trust. Planning feels more reliable than dependence. Many people confuse responsibility with control, believing faith requires self-reliance rather than surrender.

Scripture presents provision as relational, not mechanical. God provides, but not in ways that remove the need for trust. He supplies daily bread, not lifetime guarantees.

Control produces anxiety.
Trust produces peace.

Financial alignment does not eliminate planning — it removes panic. It allows people to plan wisely while trusting God as the source rather than the spreadsheet.

Scarcity Mindset and Its Long Shadow

Scarcity mindset develops when lack is experienced repeatedly. Even when circumstances improve, the mindset remains. People feel behind, anxious, and never quite secure.

Scarcity mindset says:
"There will never be enough."
"If I relax, everything will collapse."
"I have to hold tightly."

This mindset affects generosity, decision-making, and rest. It keeps people braced rather than peaceful.

God addresses scarcity mindset not by shaming it, but by reorienting trust. Provision is not just about meeting needs — it is about reshaping belief.

Abundance begins in perspective before it appears in resources.

Financial Peace Is Learned, Not Given

Financial peace is not automatic. It is learned through alignment.

Many people expect peace to arrive when income increases. Often, it does not. Without alignment, more money simply creates bigger worries.

Peace grows as habits change:
clarity replaces avoidance
planning replaces panic
discipline replaces impulse
trust replaces fear

God teaches stewardship gradually because peace must be sustainable.

Financial peace is practiced daily, not achieved instantly.

Stewardship Without Shame

Shame is one of the greatest barriers to financial healing.

People feel ashamed of debt, mistakes, lack of knowledge, or past decisions. Shame leads to avoidance, secrecy, and fear. Avoidance delays healing.

God never uses shame to teach stewardship.

Scripture addresses finances with honesty and compassion. It emphasizes wisdom, correction, and growth — not condemnation. Financial missteps do not disqualify purpose. They invite realignment.

Healing begins where honesty replaces shame.

Debt, Responsibility, and Freedom

Debt carries emotional weight. It creates pressure and limits options. Scripture treats debt cautiously because it can restrict freedom.

Freedom does not come through panic repayment or self-punishment. It comes through honest evaluation, consistent discipline, and patient progress.

God honors movement toward freedom, not perfection. Financial alignment focuses on direction rather than speed.

Debt does not define identity.
Stewardship defines direction.

Generosity and Trust

Generosity is one of the clearest expressions of financial alignment.

Not because it earns favor, but because it reveals trust. Generosity says, "God is my source." Fear says, "I must protect myself."

Generosity does not mean recklessness. It means responsiveness guided by wisdom. It adapts to season and capacity.

God values generosity that flows from peace, not pressure.

Provision in Unexpected Forms

God's provision often arrives differently than expected.

It may come as opportunity rather than cash.
As connection rather than increase.
As wisdom rather than relief.

People sometimes miss provision because they expect it to look a certain way. Alignment opens awareness to God's creative supply.

Provision is not always dramatic.
It is often faithful.

Financial Boundaries and Peace

Peace requires boundaries.

Without boundaries, finances are drained by pressure, guilt, or impulse. Saying no becomes necessary to preserve stability. Boundaries protect generosity by making it sustainable.

Jesus modeled financial boundaries. He did not meet every material need presented to Him. He acted according to assignment, not pressure.

Financial alignment honors boundaries without guilt.

Comparison and Financial Discontent

Comparison erodes financial peace quickly.

People compare income, lifestyle, progress, and opportunity. Comparison creates dissatisfaction even in provision. Gratitude fades. Anxiety increases.

God's provision is personal. Comparing paths creates unnecessary frustration. Peace grows when focus returns to stewardship rather than comparison.

Contentment does not mean lack of ambition.
It means freedom from resentment.

Trusting God in Financial Uncertainty

Uncertainty is inevitable. Markets change. Expenses arise. Income fluctuates. Trust is not the absence of uncertainty — it is confidence in God's faithfulness within it.

God does not promise financial predictability. He promises presence and provision.

Trust stabilizes the heart when numbers fluctuate.

Financial Peace Strengthens Purpose

When financial fear loosens its grip, energy returns.

Focus improves.
Decision-making clarifies.
Relationships stabilize.
Peace increases.

Purpose is easier to pursue when finances are stewarded with wisdom rather than fear.

God desires His people to live free — not enslaved by lack or obsessed with abundance.

Living Aligned With Provision

Living financially aligned means trusting God as source, stewarding resources wisely, and refusing to let fear dominate decisions.

It means money no longer defines worth, direction, or peace.

God does not promise riches.
He promises provision.

To live **Aligned for Purpose**, financial peace must replace financial fear. When provision is trusted and stewardship is practiced, peace becomes possible — not because life is perfect, but because alignment is restored.

Scriptures Referenced in This Chapter

- Matthew 6:25–34
- Philippians 4:19
- Proverbs 10:22
- Hebrews 13:5
- Luke 16:10–12
- Psalm 37:25

Chapter 20

Generational Impact: Living So Others Are Changed Because You Lived

Purpose was never meant to end with you.

One of the greatest misunderstandings about purpose is the belief that it exists solely for personal fulfillment. While purpose does bring meaning and clarity to individual life, its reach was always designed to extend beyond a single generation. God's work through a person is rarely confined to their lifetime alone. It echoes — through family, community, culture, and legacy.

Generational impact is not about fame, wealth, or recognition.
It is about **influence that outlives visibility**.

Many people underestimate the power of consistent faithfulness. They believe impact requires extraordinary moments when, in reality, it is often formed through ordinary obedience repeated over time. Words spoken in patience, boundaries honored with courage, integrity practiced quietly, and faith lived consistently shape the lives of others long after moments pass.

An aligned life creates ripple effects that reach people you may never meet.

Why Generational Impact Matters

Every person lives within a generational story. Beliefs, behaviors, fears, and values are passed down — sometimes intentionally, often unconsciously. Patterns repeat until someone interrupts them. Healing, wisdom, and faith must be practiced intentionally to change what is handed forward.

Many people inherit wounds they did not cause:
fear-based thinking
emotional distance
financial instability
spiritual confusion

Likewise, people can inherit strength they did not earn:
faithfulness
resilience
wisdom
clarity

God's design includes restoration not only for individuals, but for lineages. When one person chooses alignment, it alters the trajectory of those connected to them.

Generational impact begins when someone decides to live differently — consistently.

Breaking Cycles Through Alignment

Cycles persist until alignment interrupts them.

Cycles of anger, avoidance, addiction, scarcity, neglect, or silence are often normalized within families and communities. People learn what they see more than what they are told. Without intentional change, patterns repeat across generations.

Alignment breaks cycles because it introduces new responses. Instead of reacting from fear, aligned people respond with wisdom. Instead of avoiding pain, they process it. Instead of repeating dysfunction, they establish health.

Breaking cycles is not about blaming the past.
It is about choosing responsibility for the future.

God honors those who stand in the gap — not to condemn what was, but to redeem what will be.

The Power of Example Over Instruction

People are shaped more by observation than instruction.

Children learn faith by watching how adults respond under pressure. Communities learn values by observing how leaders handle conflict. Families learn trust by seeing consistency over time.

Words matter, but example shapes belief.

An aligned life teaches without preaching. It models patience, humility, discipline, and faithfulness in daily life. Over time, these behaviors become reference points for others.

God often uses lived example more powerfully than spoken teaching.

Legacy Is Built in Ordinary Moments

Legacy is often misunderstood as something achieved near the end of life. In reality, legacy is built daily. It is shaped by how people show up consistently, not by what they accomplish publicly.

Legacy is built when:
integrity is chosen over convenience
faith is practiced in difficulty

boundaries are honored without guilt
love is expressed with consistency

These moments rarely feel significant in isolation, yet they accumulate into influence that lasts.

God values faithfulness in the ordinary because it produces extraordinary impact over time.

Healing as a Generational Gift

Personal healing is not selfish. It is generous.

When people heal emotionally, mentally, spiritually, physically, and financially, they stop passing unresolved pain forward. They create safer environments, healthier relationships, and clearer communication for others.

Healing changes how people parent, lead, relate, and serve. It removes emotional volatility and replaces it with stability. This stability becomes a foundation for others.

God heals individuals with generations in mind.

Teaching Through Boundaries

Boundaries are a powerful generational tool.

When boundaries are practiced consistently, they teach others what is healthy. They demonstrate self-respect, discernment, and responsibility. Children raised around boundaries learn how to say no, protect their peace, and steward relationships wisely.

Boundaries do not isolate — they instruct.

Jesus modeled boundaries not to limit love, but to sustain it. When boundaries are practiced faithfully, they become generational lessons in wisdom.

Faith That Outlives You

Faith that impacts generations is not loud or performative. It is steady, sincere, and lived daily. It is visible in how challenges are faced, how failures are handled, and how hope is maintained.

Generational faith is resilient. It does not collapse under disappointment. It adapts without losing conviction.

God often works through one faithful person to restore faith across an entire lineage.

Responsibility Without Pressure

Generational impact should not feel like pressure. It is not about perfection or performance. God does not ask people to carry the weight of generations alone. He asks for obedience, not outcomes.

You do not control how others respond.
You control how you live.

Faithfulness releases responsibility for results while maintaining commitment to alignment.

God handles the outcome.
You handle obedience.

Influence Beyond Family

Generational impact extends beyond bloodlines.

Teachers, mentors, leaders, volunteers, neighbors, and friends all shape lives through influence. The way you live may become someone else's blueprint for faith, resilience, or healing.

You may never know who is watching.
You may never see the full impact.

God sees it all.

Consistency Creates Trust

Trust is the foundation of influence.

People trust what is consistent. Inconsistency erodes credibility. When faith, values, and behavior align consistently, trust grows naturally.

Generational impact depends on trust — trust that what is lived is genuine, sustainable, and real.

Consistency over time builds credibility that words alone cannot.

Leaving a Legacy of Peace

One of the greatest legacies a person can leave is peace.

Peace in how conflict is handled.
Peace in how decisions are made.
Peace in how hardship is endured.

A peaceful life becomes a refuge for others. It demonstrates trust in God rather than control over outcomes.

God's peace is contagious.

Living With Legacy in Mind

Living with generational impact in mind does not mean living in fear of mistakes. It means living with intentionality. It means choosing alignment daily, knowing your life speaks even when you are silent.

Legacy is not perfection.
It is direction.

Each aligned choice contributes to a future shaped by wisdom rather than fear.

When You Don't See the Impact

Some people never see the fruit of their faithfulness fully. Seeds are planted quietly. Growth happens later.

God honors faithfulness regardless of visibility.

What you sow today may blossom in a future you never witness. That does not make it less meaningful. It makes it eternal.

Generational Impact and Purpose

Purpose reaches its fullness when it extends beyond self.

Living aligned transforms personal life. Living aligned consistently transforms generations. God designed purpose to multiply through obedience, example, and faithfulness.

To live **Aligned for Purpose** is to live with awareness that your choices today shape the lives of others tomorrow.

Scriptures Referenced in This Chapter

- Psalm 145:4
- Proverbs 13:22
- Deuteronomy 6:6–7
- Isaiah 59:21
- 2 Timothy 1:5
- Galatians 6:9

Chapter 21

Leadership Through Service: Influence Rooted in Humility and Responsibility

True leadership is not defined by position.
It is revealed through responsibility.

Many people associate leadership with authority, visibility, or control. They assume leadership begins when someone is placed in charge or recognized publicly. God's definition of leadership is different. In His design, leadership begins long before a title is given and continues long after recognition fades.

Leadership is influence carried with humility.

An aligned life understands that leadership is not about elevating self, but about stewarding responsibility well. It is not measured by how many people follow you, but by how faithfully you serve those entrusted to you. Purpose often unfolds through leadership expressed quietly, consistently, and sacrificially.

God entrusts leadership to those who are willing to serve without demanding status.

Why Leadership Often Gets Distorted

Leadership becomes distorted when it is driven by ego rather than stewardship.

When people pursue leadership for validation, power, or control, influence becomes toxic. Decisions are shaped by image rather than integrity. People are used instead of served. Over time, trust erodes and damage follows.

Scripture consistently warns against self-centered leadership because it misrepresents God's heart. Leadership rooted in pride creates pressure and division. Leadership rooted in humility creates stability and growth.

God's model of leadership is not self-promotion.
It is responsibility accepted with reverence.

Service as the Foundation of Leadership

In God's design, service precedes leadership.

Before authority is entrusted, faithfulness is tested. Before influence is expanded, character is examined. Service reveals motive. It exposes whether someone desires impact or attention.

Serving without recognition refines humility. Serving consistently builds trust. Serving sacrificially strengthens character.

Leadership that grows out of service is sustainable. Leadership pursued without service collapses under pressure.

God elevates those who serve faithfully where they are.

Responsibility Without Entitlement

One of the clearest markers of aligned leadership is responsibility without entitlement.

Entitlement demands reward for effort. Responsibility accepts duty without expectation of applause. Leaders who operate with entitlement grow resentful when appreciation is lacking. Leaders who operate with responsibility remain steady regardless of recognition.

God does not promise affirmation for every act of leadership. He promises fruit over time.

Leadership becomes heavy when entitlement grows. It becomes meaningful when responsibility is embraced.

Leading Without Control

Control is often mistaken for leadership.

Controlling leaders micromanage, dominate decisions, and resist accountability. They believe outcomes depend entirely on them. This mindset creates exhaustion — both for the leader and for those under their influence.

God's leadership model is relational, not controlling. It guides rather than dominates. It empowers rather than suppresses. It trusts rather than manipulates.

Leadership rooted in trust builds confidence in others. Leadership rooted in control builds fear.

Aligned leaders release control and embrace stewardship.

Leadership Under Pressure

Pressure reveals leadership maturity.

When stress increases, true leadership surfaces. Some react with defensiveness. Others withdraw. Aligned leaders remain grounded. They do not panic, blame, or abandon responsibility. They respond with wisdom.

Pressure exposes whether leadership is rooted in ego or alignment. Ego seeks to protect image. Alignment seeks to protect people and purpose.

God develops leaders through pressure because pressure refines discernment and strengthens dependence on Him.

Humility as Strength

Humility is not weakness.
It is clarity about one's role.

Humble leaders understand that influence is entrusted, not earned. They recognize their limitations and seek wisdom rather than pretending competence. Humility creates teachability. Teachability sustains growth.

God resists pride because pride resists correction. He honors humility because humility remains aligned.

Leadership without humility becomes dangerous. Leadership with humility becomes transformative.

Serving People, Not Using Them

Aligned leadership values people over outcomes.

When people become means to an end, leadership loses integrity. God's leadership model places people at the center. Outcomes matter, but not at the expense of dignity, well-being, or truth.

Serving leaders listen. They observe. They respond thoughtfully rather than reactively. They correct without humiliation and guide without manipulation.

Leadership rooted in service builds loyalty, trust, and health.

Leadership and Boundaries

Healthy leadership requires boundaries.

Without boundaries, leaders burn out or become resentful. Overextension weakens clarity and decision-making. Saying yes to everything diminishes effectiveness.

Jesus modeled boundaries consistently. He withdrew from crowds. He delegated responsibility. He honored rest. These boundaries preserved His effectiveness and protected His mission.

Aligned leaders understand that boundaries do not limit leadership — they sustain it.

Integrity as the Anchor of Influence

Integrity is the foundation of lasting leadership.

Influence without integrity collapses eventually. Integrity aligns words with actions, promises with follow-through, and values with behavior. People trust leaders whose lives reflect consistency.

God values integrity because it reflects truth. Leadership rooted in integrity does not require constant defense. Its consistency speaks for itself.

Integrity builds influence quietly but powerfully.

Leadership That Develops Others

Aligned leadership multiplies rather than hoards influence.

Rather than securing position, healthy leaders invest in others. They mentor, empower, and prepare others to lead responsibly. They understand that leadership is not diminished by shared responsibility — it is strengthened by it.

God's design for leadership includes multiplication, not dependence.

Leaders who develop others leave sustainable impact.

Leadership Without Applause

Much of leadership happens without recognition.

Decisions made quietly. Sacrifices unseen. Responsibilities carried without acknowledgment. Leadership rooted in service remains faithful regardless of visibility.

God sees what others overlook. He honors faithfulness done in obscurity.

Leadership without applause tests motive and strengthens humility.

When Leadership Feels Heavy

Leadership can feel heavy at times.

Responsibility weighs. Expectations press. Decisions carry consequence. Aligned leaders do not deny this weight. They bring it to God rather than carrying it alone.

God does not expect leaders to be invincible. He expects them to be dependent.

Leadership becomes lighter when surrendered to God.

Servant Leadership and Purpose

Purpose is often expressed through leadership roles — in families, workplaces, ministries, and communities. Servant leadership ensures that purpose blesses rather than burdens others.

Leadership rooted in service aligns influence with God's heart.

God does not measure leadership by scale.
He measures it by faithfulness.

Living as a Servant Leader

Living as a servant leader means embracing responsibility with humility, integrity, and care. It means influencing others through example rather than force.

When leadership is aligned:
trust grows
people flourish
decisions stabilize
purpose expands

God designed leadership to be a reflection of His character — loving, wise, and just.

To live **Aligned for Purpose**, leadership must be rooted in service rather than status. When leadership flows from humility and responsibility, influence becomes redemptive rather than destructive.

Scriptures Referenced in This Chapter

- Mark 10:42–45
- Matthew 23:11–12
- Philippians 2:3–4
- Proverbs 11:2
- 1 Peter 5:2–3
- Luke 12:48

Chapter 22

Accountability and Integrity: Living the Same in Private as in Public

Integrity is revealed most clearly where no one is watching.

Many people value integrity in theory, yet struggle with consistency in practice. They live one way publicly and another privately, not always out of malice, but out of fatigue, fear, or pressure. Over time, this divide creates inner conflict. Peace weakens. Confidence erodes. Life begins to feel fragmented.

God never designed life to be divided.

Integrity is alignment — the quiet agreement between belief and behavior, conviction and conduct, private decisions and public actions. Accountability protects this alignment by bringing truth into the light. Together, integrity and accountability form a foundation that sustains purpose over time.

An aligned life cannot thrive without them.

Why Integrity Matters More Than Image

Image manages perception.
Integrity governs reality.

Image asks how things look. Integrity asks how things are. Many people prioritize image because it offers immediate validation. Integrity often offers none. It demands consistency even when recognition is absent.

God values integrity because it reflects truth. Truth does not shift with circumstance. When integrity is compromised, internal tension grows. People feel unsettled without knowing why. Peace fades not because life is difficult, but because life is misaligned.

Integrity restores peace by removing inner contradiction.

The Quiet Power of Private Choices

Private choices shape public outcomes.

The decisions made alone — how time is used, how thoughts are managed, how boundaries are honored — determine the strength of character revealed later. Public success without private integrity eventually collapses under its own weight.

God prepares people privately before using them publicly. What is built in secret sustains what becomes visible.

Private obedience creates public stability.

Accountability as Protection, Not Punishment

Accountability is often misunderstood as control or mistrust. In God's design, accountability is protection. It guards against self-deception, rationalization, and isolation.

Everyone has blind spots. Accountability brings perspective. It invites correction before damage occurs. It strengthens discernment by introducing wisdom beyond personal perception.

God places accountability in relationships because isolation breeds distortion.

Accountability does not weaken freedom.
It preserves it.

Why Accountability Is Resisted

Many resist accountability because it feels vulnerable.

Being accountable requires honesty, humility, and openness. It removes the illusion of self-sufficiency. For those who have been hurt by authority or betrayal, accountability can feel threatening.

However, refusing accountability often leads to isolation, not safety. Without accountability, rationalization grows. Justification replaces truth. Over time, misalignment becomes normalized.

God invites accountability because He values wholeness, not exposure.

Integrity Under Pressure

Pressure tests integrity.

When stakes are high and stress increases, shortcuts become tempting. People justify compromise in the name of urgency, survival, or necessity. These moments reveal whether integrity is conditional or consistent.

God does not remove pressure to make integrity easier. He strengthens conviction so integrity remains intact within pressure.

Integrity under pressure builds confidence.
Compromise under pressure erodes trust.

Small Compromises and Long-Term Cost

Integrity is rarely lost in a single moment. It erodes gradually through small compromises.

One rationalized decision.
One unspoken truth.
One boundary ignored.

These compromises feel insignificant individually, yet they accumulate. Over time, alignment weakens and peace fades. People feel unsettled without knowing why.

God addresses compromise early because He values restoration over consequence.

Integrity preserved early prevents regret later.

Living Without Double Standards

Double standards fracture integrity.

Holding others to expectations not practiced personally creates hypocrisy. Over time, credibility diminishes. Influence weakens. Relationships strain.

God calls for consistent standards — not perfection, but honesty. Integrity does not demand flawlessness. It demands sincerity.

People trust those who live transparently, not those who appear flawless.

The Role of Confession and Correction

Confession restores integrity.

Admitting error does not weaken credibility — it strengthens it. Confession interrupts denial and invites healing. God honors honesty because it creates space for correction and growth.

Correction is not rejection. It is refinement.

An aligned life receives correction without defensiveness. It views correction as an opportunity to realign rather than an attack to resist.

Integrity in Leadership and Influence

Integrity becomes increasingly important as influence grows.

Leadership without integrity damages trust. Influence without accountability creates harm. God holds leaders to higher standards not to burden them, but to protect those they serve.

Aligned leadership invites accountability rather than resisting it. It welcomes feedback and correction. Integrity strengthens influence by anchoring it in truth.

Accountability in Relationships

Healthy relationships include accountability.

Friends, mentors, spouses, and community members help one another stay aligned. Accountability spoken in love strengthens trust rather than threatening it.

God designed relationships to support growth. Isolation weakens integrity by removing perspective.

Accountability spoken gently preserves connection.

Integrity and Long-Term Peace

Integrity produces peace that circumstances cannot remove.

Life may still be difficult. Challenges may remain. But internal peace stabilizes when integrity is intact. There is no hidden fear of exposure. No inner conflict between belief and behavior.

Peace flows from alignment.

God's peace rests on those who live honestly before Him.

Accountability Without Shame

God never uses accountability to shame.

Shame hides. Accountability reveals. Shame isolates. Accountability restores. God corrects with compassion, not condemnation.

An aligned life embraces accountability as a tool for growth rather than a threat to worth.

Correction guided by love strengthens identity.

Integrity Across All Areas of Life

Integrity is holistic.

It includes spiritual faithfulness, emotional honesty, mental discipline, physical stewardship, relational truthfulness, and financial responsibility. Integrity does not compartmentalize. It aligns life fully.

When integrity is practiced consistently, life feels whole rather than fragmented.

God desires wholeness, not performance.

Living an Accountable Life

Living with accountability means inviting trusted voices into your life, remaining teachable, and choosing truth over comfort.

It means asking:
"Does my private life support my public values?"
"Am I living honestly before God and others?"
"Am I open to correction?"

These questions protect alignment.

Integrity as a Legacy

Integrity leaves a legacy of trust.

People remember consistency long after achievements fade. Integrity shapes families, organizations, and communities. It teaches others what alignment looks like in practice.

God values integrity because it multiplies faithfulness across generations.

Living Aligned Through Integrity

To live **Aligned for Purpose** means choosing integrity daily — in thought, word, and action — and embracing accountability as protection rather than threat.

Integrity sustains purpose.
Accountability preserves alignment.

Together, they form a life that remains steady, peaceful, and trustworthy in every season.

Scriptures Referenced in This Chapter

- Proverbs 10:9
- Psalm 51:6
- Luke 16:10
- Proverbs 27:17
- 1 John 1:7
- Titus 2:7

Chapter 23

Community and Connection: Thriving Through God-Centered Relationships

No one is designed to walk alone.

From the beginning, God's design for humanity included connection. Purpose was never meant to be carried in isolation, nor was growth intended to happen without relationship. Yet many people today live disconnected lives — surrounded by people but emotionally isolated, busy yet lonely, involved yet unseen.

God did not design community as a convenience.
He designed it as a **necessity**.

An aligned life understands that community is not optional to purpose. It is foundational. Connection strengthens faith, stabilizes identity, sharpens discernment, and provides support in seasons of weakness. Without healthy community, even the strongest individuals become vulnerable to burnout, discouragement, and distortion.

Purpose flourishes best where connection is present.

Why Isolation Has Become So Common

Isolation often develops quietly.

It grows through disappointment, betrayal, busyness, or survival. People withdraw after being hurt. They become self-reliant after being let down. They prioritize productivity over relationship because connection feels complicated or costly.

Over time, independence becomes a shield.

Isolation says:
"I don't want to be disappointed again."
"I'm safer handling things myself."
"I don't have time for relationships."

While isolation may feel protective, it slowly erodes emotional health, spiritual clarity, and resilience. God never intended self-reliance to replace community.

Strength grows through connection, not avoidance.

Community as God's Design for Growth

God uses community to shape character.

Relationships expose blind spots, test humility, and develop patience. They provide encouragement during discouragement and correction when alignment drifts. Community is not merely social — it is spiritual.

Scripture consistently shows God working through people to refine people. Wisdom flows through counsel. Strength is shared through support. Healing often occurs through relationship.

Community does what isolation cannot:
it reflects truth back to us.

God designed connection to protect people from self-deception and discouragement.

The Difference Between Proximity and Connection

Many people confuse proximity with connection.

Being around people does not guarantee relationship. Genuine connection requires vulnerability, trust, and consistency. Without these, relationships remain surface-level and unsustaining.

God-centered community is marked by honesty, grace, accountability, and shared values. It does not demand perfection. It requires sincerity.

True connection allows people to be seen without fear of rejection.

Healthy Community Versus Harmful Dependence

Community must be healthy to be sustaining.

Healthy community supports growth without creating dependence. It encourages responsibility while offering support. It allows individuals to remain whole rather than dissolving identity into the group.

Unhealthy community creates pressure, conformity, or emotional reliance. God's design for community preserves individuality while fostering unity.

Connection should strengthen purpose, not replace it.

Vulnerability as the Doorway to Connection

Vulnerability makes connection possible.

Without honesty, relationships remain guarded. Without openness, trust cannot grow. Vulnerability does not mean oversharing — it means being truthful and present.

Many people fear vulnerability because it risks rejection. God honors vulnerability because it invites healing. Scripture repeatedly shows God meeting people where they are honest, not where they pretend.

Vulnerability transforms connection from transactional to transformational.

Community and Emotional Resilience

Community strengthens emotional resilience.

Shared burdens become lighter. Perspective widens. Encouragement restores hope. When people walk alone, struggles feel heavier and more overwhelming.

God designed community to help carry emotional weight. Support does not remove hardship — it makes it manageable.

Resilience grows faster in community than in isolation.

Discernment in Choosing Community

Not every group qualifies as healthy community.

God calls for discernment in relationships. Alignment matters. Values matter. Character matters. Community should reinforce truth, not undermine it.

Healthy community encourages growth, accountability, and peace. Harmful community amplifies fear, compromise, or pressure.

God does not ask people to connect indiscriminately. He invites intentional connection.

Community During Difficult Seasons

Difficult seasons reveal the value of community.

During hardship, people often withdraw out of shame or fatigue. Yet this is when connection is most needed. God often uses community to provide support, clarity, and strength during adversity.

Allowing others to walk with you during difficulty is not weakness — it is wisdom.

God's provision often comes through people.

Serving One Another in Community

Community is not only about receiving. It is about giving.

Serving one another builds mutual respect and shared responsibility. When people serve together, connection deepens. Purpose expands. Community becomes active rather than passive.

God designed community to function through contribution, not consumption.

Serving strengthens belonging.

Forgiveness and Grace in Community

Community requires grace.

People disappoint. Misunderstandings occur. Conflict arises. Without forgiveness, community fractures. God's design includes grace because relationship cannot survive perfectionism.

Forgiveness restores connection. Grace allows growth. Without them, isolation becomes inevitable.

Healthy community practices forgiveness without ignoring truth.

Community as a Place of Accountability

Accountability strengthens community.

Healthy community encourages truth, correction, and alignment. Accountability is not control — it is care. It protects individuals from drifting while preserving dignity.

God designed accountability to be relational rather than hierarchical. It flows from trust rather than authority.

Accountability practiced in love strengthens connection.

Community Beyond Comfort Zones

God-centered community often stretches comfort.

It brings together people of different backgrounds, experiences, and perspectives. This diversity refines humility and broadens understanding. God uses diversity to strengthen unity.

Growth often happens beyond familiarity.

Community expands perspective.

Longevity Through Connection

Purpose requires endurance. Endurance requires support.

Those who attempt to carry calling alone often burn out prematurely. Community provides encouragement that sustains long journeys.

God designed community to preserve longevity, not merely companionship.

Connection sustains faithfulness.

Leaving Isolation Behind

Leaving isolation requires courage.

It means risking disappointment, trusting again, and choosing connection despite past hurt. God heals relational wounds not by avoiding relationships, but by restoring healthy ones.

Healing often comes through re-engagement.

God restores through connection.

Living Connected and Aligned

Living an aligned life means valuing community intentionally. It means investing time, honesty, and effort into relationships that support growth.

When community is healthy:
faith deepens
clarity increases
resilience strengthens
purpose flourishes

God does not call people to walk alone.
He calls them to walk **together**.

To live **Aligned for Purpose**, community and connection must be embraced as essential, not optional. God-centered relationships protect alignment, sustain growth, and ensure purpose is lived with strength and support.

Scriptures Referenced in This Chapter

- Ecclesiastes 4:9–12
- Hebrews 10:24–25
- Proverbs 27:17
- Romans 12:10
- Galatians 6:2
- Psalm 133:1

Chapter 24

Healing and Restoration: Allowing God to Repair What Life Has Wounded

Healing is not forgetting.
It is restoration.

Many people live productive, faithful, and outwardly stable lives while quietly carrying unresolved wounds. Pain is buried beneath responsibility. Trauma is masked by strength. Loss is managed through distraction. Over time, what is unhealed begins to shape behavior, relationships, and perception.

God never intended wounds to be permanent.

Healing is not a denial of pain. It is the process of allowing God to restore what has been damaged by experience, betrayal, loss, neglect, or disappointment. Restoration does not erase the past — it redeems it. An aligned life understands that healing is not optional to purpose; it is foundational.

Purpose cannot be carried well through unhealed places.

Why Healing Is Often Delayed

Healing is delayed not because people do not want it, but because healing requires exposure.

To heal, pain must be acknowledged. Memories must be revisited. Emotions must be named. For many, this feels unsafe. God understands this hesitation. He does not force healing; He invites it.

Many delay healing because:
pain has become familiar
strength is mistaken for wholeness
busyness masks discomfort
fear of reopening wounds persists

Ignoring wounds does not remove them. It allows them to operate unseen. God calls wounds into the light not to shame, but to restore.

Healing begins where honesty replaces avoidance.

The Difference Between Coping and Healing

Coping manages symptoms.
Healing restores function.

Many people cope well. They function, succeed, and serve while remaining internally wounded. Coping strategies may include distraction, productivity, humor, isolation, or emotional detachment. While coping can be necessary temporarily, it cannot replace healing.

Healing addresses the root. It restores emotional responsiveness, relational safety, and internal peace. God does not desire people to merely cope with life — He desires them to live whole.

Coping keeps pain contained.
Healing transforms it.

Healing Requires Safety

God heals gently.

Healing occurs where safety is present — safety in relationship, environment, and pacing. God does not rush restoration. He meets people where they are ready, not where they feel pressured to be.

Safety includes:
permission to feel
freedom to speak truth
absence of condemnation
respect for boundaries

God creates safety through His presence. Healing unfolds in trust, not force.

The Role of Grief in Healing

Grief is a necessary companion to healing.

Loss must be mourned — not only loss of people, but loss of innocence, trust, opportunity, or expectation. Unacknowledged grief hardens into bitterness or numbness.

God invites grief because it opens space for comfort. Scripture repeatedly shows God near to the brokenhearted. Grief honors what was lost while allowing restoration to begin.

Healing does not bypass grief.
It passes through it.

Forgiveness as Release, Not Excuse

Forgiveness is often misunderstood.

Forgiveness does not minimize harm. It does not excuse wrongdoing. It does not require reconciliation in unsafe situations. Forgiveness is release — releasing the burden of carrying resentment and allowing God to handle justice.

Unforgiveness binds people to the wound. Forgiveness frees the wounded from ongoing captivity.

God invites forgiveness not to protect offenders, but to heal the wounded.

Healing and the Body

Trauma is stored in the body.

Stress, anxiety, and unresolved pain often manifest physically — tension, fatigue, illness, or chronic discomfort. God designed healing to include the body, not bypass it.

Rest, nourishment, movement, and gentleness support healing. Ignoring physical signals slows restoration.

God cares for the body as part of wholeness.

Healing Does Not Erase Memory

Healing changes how memory functions.

Memories may remain, but their power diminishes. Pain no longer dictates reaction. Triggers lose intensity. Perspective shifts.

God does not erase memory to heal. He redeems memory by removing its control.

Healing allows the past to inform without imprisoning.

Healing Requires Patience

Healing is rarely linear.

Progress may feel uneven. Breakthroughs may be followed by setbacks. This is normal. God does not measure healing by speed. He values sincerity and perseverance.

Patience protects healing from pressure. Rushing restoration can reopen wounds.

God heals thoroughly, not hurriedly.

Community in the Healing Process

Healing is often supported through community.

Trusted relationships provide perspective, validation, and safety. Isolation slows healing by limiting reflection and support. God frequently uses people as instruments of restoration.

Healthy community does not rush healing. It walks alongside it.

God heals through presence — His and others'.

Healing and Identity

Wounds distort identity.

Unhealed pain can cause people to see themselves as broken, unworthy, or unsafe. Healing restores true identity — one rooted in God rather than experience.

God heals not only pain, but perception.

Restored identity strengthens confidence and peace.

Healing Prepares You for Purpose

Healing is preparation.

Unhealed wounds leak into leadership, relationships, decision-making, and service. Healing strengthens capacity to carry responsibility without projection or reactivity.

God heals so purpose can be lived without harm to self or others.

Healing does not delay purpose.
It protects it.

Restoration Is God's Nature

God is a restorer.

Scripture consistently portrays Him as one who rebuilds, renews, and redeems. He restores what was stolen, broken, or lost. Restoration does not always look like replacement — it looks like transformation.

God specializes in turning wounds into wisdom.

Choosing to Heal

Healing requires a choice.

God offers restoration, but He does not force it. Choosing healing means choosing honesty, patience, and trust. It means releasing the identity formed by pain and embracing the identity formed by God.

This choice may need to be made repeatedly.

Healing is a journey, not a moment.

Living Restored

Living restored does not mean pain never resurfaces. It means pain no longer governs life. It means responding rather than reacting, trusting rather than guarding, and living open rather than braced.

Restoration brings peace where tension once lived.

Healing as a Testimony

Healed lives testify quietly.

People notice stability, compassion, and wisdom that emerge from restoration. Healing does not make people perfect — it makes them authentic.

God uses healed lives to offer hope to others.

Living Aligned Through Healing

To live **Aligned for Purpose** means allowing God to heal what life has wounded. Healing restores capacity, strengthens relationships, and preserves peace. It allows purpose to be lived from wholeness rather than pain.

God does not waste wounds.
He restores them.

Scriptures Referenced in This Chapter

- Psalm 147:3
- Isaiah 61:1–3
- Jeremiah 30:17
- Matthew 11:28–30
- 2 Corinthians 5:17
- Joel 2:25

Chapter 25

Identity and Worth: Living From Who God Says You Are

Identity shapes everything.

It determines how people interpret experiences, make decisions, handle conflict, pursue purpose, and respond to pressure. When identity is unclear, life feels unstable. When identity is rooted, life gains direction. Many people struggle not because they lack faith or discipline, but because they are living from identities shaped by pain, performance, or expectation rather than truth.

God never intended identity to be earned.
He designed it to be received.

An aligned life begins with identity anchored in God's declaration, not human approval. Worth is not produced by success, usefulness, or recognition. It is established by God and affirmed through relationship with Him. Purpose flows best from identity, not toward it.

Why Identity Becomes Distorted

Identity becomes distorted through experience.

Pain teaches false narratives. Rejection shapes belief. Failure whispers lies. Comparison magnifies insecurity. Over time, people internalize these messages until they feel factual.

Common identity distortions include:
"I am only valuable when I perform."
"I am defined by my past."
"I am replaceable."
"I am not enough."

These beliefs influence behavior quietly but powerfully. They affect boundaries, relationships, ambition, and rest. God addresses identity distortion not by demanding change, but by revealing truth.

Healing identity begins with exposure to truth.

Performance-Based Identity

Performance-based identity ties worth to output.

People who live this way feel valuable when they are productive and invisible when they are not. Rest feels guilty. Saying no feels dangerous. Failure feels catastrophic.

Performance-based identity is exhausting because worth must be constantly proven. Even success does not satisfy — it only raises the bar.

God never designed worth to be sustained by effort.
He designed it to be secure in relationship.

Performance may be appreciated, but it does not establish value.

Identity Shaped by Pain

Pain imprints identity deeply.

Trauma, betrayal, neglect, and loss shape how people see themselves and the world. Wounds create protective identities — the strong one, the invisible one, the caretaker, the overachiever. These identities form to survive pain, but they often remain long after danger has passed.

God honors survival, but He invites restoration.

Healing identity does not deny pain. It redefines self beyond it. God does not call people to remain defined by what hurt them.

Pain informs experience.
It does not define identity.

God's Declaration of Identity

God declares identity clearly in Scripture.

People are described as loved, chosen, redeemed, adopted, and purposeful. These declarations are not conditional. They are not earned. They are rooted in God's character rather than human performance.

Identity in God is received through relationship, not achieved through effort.

When identity is rooted in God's declaration, peace increases. Comparison fades. Confidence stabilizes. Purpose clarifies.

Truth restores identity.

Living From Identity, Not Toward It

Many people live toward identity.

They strive to prove worth, earn validation, and secure belonging. This approach reverses God's design. It places identity at the end of effort rather than at the beginning.

God invites people to live **from** identity.

When identity is secure:
boundaries strengthen
decisions clarify
relationships stabilize
rest becomes possible

Purpose flows naturally from identity rather than competing with it.

Identity and Boundaries

Healthy identity produces healthy boundaries.

When people know who they are, they do not fear saying no. They do not overextend to gain approval. They do not compromise values to maintain belonging.

Boundaries protect identity from erosion. God honors boundaries because they preserve wholeness.

Identity rooted in God does not need constant validation.

Identity in Relationships

Identity influences how people relate.

Insecure identity seeks validation through people. Secure identity offers connection without dependence. When identity is unclear, relationships become transactional. When identity is rooted, relationships become mutual.

God-centered identity allows people to love without losing self.

Healthy relationships require identity clarity.

Comparison and Identity Erosion

Comparison erodes identity quickly.

Comparing achievements, appearance, progress, or calling creates distortion. People forget their unique assignment and measure themselves against others' journeys.

God's design is individual, not competitive.

Comparison replaces gratitude with insecurity. Identity rooted in God resists comparison because it knows assignment is personal.

Purpose is not duplicated.
Identity is not transferable.

Identity and Calling

Calling flows from identity.

When calling is pursued without identity clarity, people attach worth to outcome. When calling is pursued from identity, effort becomes joyful rather than desperate.

God reveals calling after identity is anchored so purpose does not become a substitute for worth.

Identity precedes assignment.

Renewing the Mind to Restore Identity

Identity is reinforced through thought patterns.

False beliefs must be challenged repeatedly. Renewal takes time. God restores identity through truth applied consistently.

Replacing lies with truth is an intentional process. Scripture renews perspective. Reflection reveals distortion. Community affirms truth.

Identity is strengthened through repetition of truth.

Identity During Failure

Failure tests identity.

When failure occurs, people with performance-based identity collapse internally. Shame grows. Confidence fades. People with God-centered identity experience disappointment without devastation.

Failure does not change identity.
It reveals growth areas.

God uses failure to refine character, not redefine worth.

Identity and Rest

Rest reveals identity.

Those rooted in God rest without guilt. Those rooted in performance struggle to stop. Rest becomes a spiritual act of trust — trusting worth remains even in stillness.

God invites rest to reinforce identity beyond effort.

Rest declares trust in God's provision.

Living Securely in Identity

Secure identity produces stability.

People become less reactive, less defensive, and more discerning. They respond thoughtfully rather than impulsively. Identity rooted in God steadies the soul.

Security is not arrogance.
It is clarity.

God-centered identity allows people to stand firm without comparison or fear.

Identity as a Gift to Others

Secure identity blesses others.

It creates safety in relationships. It reduces competition. It encourages collaboration. People feel seen rather than used.

God restores identity not only for individuals, but for community.

Wholeness multiplies.

Choosing to Live From Truth

Living from identity requires intentional choice.

God's truth must be believed repeatedly, especially when feelings contradict it. Identity grows stronger through obedience to truth rather than agreement with emotion.

Truth remains stable even when feelings fluctuate.

Living Aligned Through Identity

To live **Aligned for Purpose** means anchoring identity and worth in God's declaration rather than human validation. Identity rooted in God produces peace, clarity, and confidence that sustain purpose through every season.

You do not have to become worthy.
You already are.

Scriptures Referenced in This Chapter

- Genesis 1:27
- Romans 8:15–17
- Ephesians 1:4–5
- Psalm 139:13–14
- 1 Peter 2:9
- 2 Corinthians 5:17

Chapter 26

Resilience Through Change: Remaining Aligned When Life Shifts

Change is inevitable.
Misalignment is not.

Life rarely unfolds exactly as planned. Seasons shift. Roles change. Relationships evolve. Opportunities open and close. What once felt stable may suddenly feel uncertain. Change can be exciting, painful, disorienting, or all three at once. Yet change itself is not the enemy of purpose. Resistance to change often is.

God never promised a static life.
He promised faithful presence through every transition.

An aligned life is not one that avoids change, but one that remains anchored through it. Resilience allows people to move through change without losing identity, faith, or direction. It enables adaptation without compromise and flexibility without fragmentation.

Purpose does not disappear during change.
It is often clarified by it.

Why Change Feels So Disruptive

Change disrupts familiarity.

Familiarity provides a sense of safety, even when it is imperfect. When change occurs, routines are interrupted, expectations are challenged, and control feels threatened. The mind interprets uncertainty as risk, triggering fear or resistance.

Many people struggle with change because they equate stability with security. God offers a deeper security — one rooted in His character rather than circumstances.

When security is external, change feels dangerous.
When security is internal, change becomes navigable.

The Difference Between Adaptation and Compromise

Resilience requires adaptation, not compromise.

Adaptation adjusts methods while preserving values. Compromise sacrifices values to reduce discomfort. During change, people often confuse the two. They adjust behaviors in ways that quietly erode integrity.

God invites adaptation that maintains alignment.

Resilient people ask:
"What must change?"
"What must remain?"

Values remain. Convictions remain. Purpose remains. Only expression shifts. This distinction protects alignment during transition.

Change Reveals What Is Anchoring You

Change exposes foundations.

When circumstances shift, whatever identity, peace, or confidence was resting on those circumstances is shaken. This exposure can be unsettling, but it is also clarifying.

If peace disappears during change, it may have been anchored to stability rather than God. If identity fractures, it may have been attached to role rather than relationship.

God uses change to reveal misplaced anchors — not to shame, but to restore alignment.

Resilience Is Not Resistance

Resilience is not stubbornness.

Resisting change often increases suffering. It keeps people clinging to what no longer fits, draining energy and prolonging grief. Resilience accepts reality without surrendering hope.

Resilient people grieve what is lost while remaining open to what is forming. They do not deny pain, but they do not allow pain to define direction.

God honors honesty in transition.

Letting Go Without Losing Yourself

One of the greatest challenges in change is letting go.

Letting go of roles, routines, expectations, or identities that once provided meaning can feel like losing self. God reassures people that identity is not lost in letting go — it is refined.

What ends does not erase who you are.
It reveals who you are becoming.

God often removes what no longer serves purpose to make space for deeper alignment.

Resilience and Emotional Regulation

Change intensifies emotion.

Anxiety rises. Grief surfaces. Excitement mixes with fear. Resilience does not suppress emotion — it processes it wisely. Emotional regulation allows people to experience change without becoming overwhelmed by it.

God designed emotions as signals, not leaders. Resilient people acknowledge emotions while anchoring decisions in truth.

Stability comes from alignment, not emotional certainty.

Change Without Identity Loss

Identity loss is one of the greatest risks during change.

When identity is tied to role, position, or season, transition creates crisis. When identity is rooted in God, change becomes an adjustment rather than a collapse.

God never ties identity to season.
He ties it to relationship.

Resilient identity allows people to remain whole while circumstances shift.

Trusting God's Direction When the Path Changes

Unexpected change often feels like detour.

People question whether they missed God's will or made wrong choices. Scripture shows that God's direction includes redirection. Closed doors do not always indicate failure. Sometimes they signal protection or preparation.

God's guidance is not linear.
It is intentional.

Trust deepens when direction shifts without explanation. Faith grows when obedience continues despite uncertainty.

Resilience Is Built Before Change Arrives

Resilience is not developed during crisis alone.

It is built through daily alignment — consistent faith, emotional awareness, physical care, mental clarity, and spiritual discipline. These practices strengthen the inner framework needed to navigate change.

Those who live aligned regularly adapt more easily when disruption occurs.

Preparation happens quietly long before change becomes visible.

Community and Resilience

Resilience is strengthened through connection.

Isolation magnifies uncertainty. Community provides perspective, encouragement, and grounding. God often uses relationships to stabilize people during transition.

Sharing the journey does not weaken resilience — it reinforces it.

God designed community as support during change.

Learning to Move Forward Without Clarity

Change often removes clarity.

Plans dissolve. Direction feels blurred. Resilience allows people to move forward without full understanding. Faithfulness replaces foresight. Obedience replaces certainty.

God does not require clarity before movement.
He requires trust.

Each step taken in faith builds momentum even when the destination is unknown.

Growth Hidden Within Change

Change often hides growth.

Skills develop. Character deepens. Perspective widens. These changes may not be immediately visible, but they are foundational. God often uses transition to shape people internally before shifting them externally.

What feels like disruption may be development.

Resilience Prevents Bitterness

Without resilience, change can breed bitterness.

Resentment grows when loss is unprocessed or when expectations remain rigid. Resilience allows acceptance without resignation. It keeps the heart open rather than hardened.

God heals disappointment through trust, not denial.

Staying Aligned Through Transition

Alignment during change requires intentional recalibration.

Routines may adjust. Priorities may shift. Boundaries may change. Alignment asks, "What does faithfulness look like now?" rather than clinging to what no longer fits.

God's design allows alignment to evolve without breaking.

Change as Invitation

God often uses change as invitation.

An invitation to deepen trust.
To refine purpose.
To strengthen faith.
To release what no longer serves growth.

Change invites reflection rather than panic.

God is present in transition.

Living Resiliently Aligned

Living resiliently does not mean avoiding pain. It means remaining anchored while moving forward. It means trusting God's faithfulness through uncertainty and allowing alignment to guide adaptation.

Resilience protects purpose by preventing collapse during transition.

To live **Aligned for Purpose**, resilience through change must be embraced as strength, not weakness. God does not abandon people in change — He walks with them through it, shaping maturity, stability, and deeper trust.

Scriptures Referenced in This Chapter

- Isaiah 43:18–19
- Proverbs 3:5–6
- Ecclesiastes 3:1
- James 1:2–4
- Psalm 37:23–24
- 2 Corinthians 4:16–18

Chapter 27

Living With Discernment in a Confused World

Confusion is no longer the exception in modern life — it has become the environment.

Information is constant, opinions are loud, truth is often blurred, and values shift depending on convenience or popularity. People are no longer simply choosing between right and wrong; they are choosing between competing versions of "truth," each claiming authority, urgency, and moral superiority. In such a world, discernment is not optional. It is essential for survival, stability, and purpose.

Discernment is the ability to see clearly when clarity is rare. It is the skill of recognizing what aligns with God's truth when noise is overwhelming. Without discernment, people react instead of respond, follow trends instead of conviction, and make decisions rooted in pressure rather than wisdom. Over time, confusion erodes confidence, fractures identity, and weakens faith.

God never intended His people to live disoriented.

An aligned life depends on discernment because purpose cannot be sustained where perception is distorted. Discernment protects the mind, guards the heart, and anchors decisions in truth rather than emotion, culture, or fear.

Why Confusion Is So Powerful Today

Confusion thrives where information is abundant but wisdom is scarce.

People are exposed to endless content — news, commentary, advice, social media, spiritual opinions, and conflicting values — yet rarely taught how to evaluate what they consume. The mind becomes overloaded. Attention fractures. Emotional responses intensify. In this environment, people often mistake urgency for importance and popularity for truth.

Confusion feels overwhelming because it demands constant decision-making without clear standards. When truth is relative, every choice becomes exhausting. People grow anxious not because they lack intelligence, but because they lack discernment.

God's design provides clarity not by simplifying the world, but by anchoring people internally so they are not ruled by external chaos.

Discernment Is Not Suspicion

Discernment is often confused with skepticism or cynicism. In reality, discernment is not distrust — it is clarity. Suspicion assumes harm everywhere. Discernment evaluates carefully without fear. Cynicism closes the heart. Discernment keeps it open but guarded.

Discernment requires humility. It acknowledges that not everything labeled "good," "right," or even "spiritual" is aligned with God's truth. It also recognizes that not everything uncomfortable is wrong. Growth often challenges comfort.

Godly discernment seeks alignment, not validation.

The Difference Between Knowledge and Wisdom

Knowledge gathers information.
Wisdom applies truth.

Many people are knowledgeable yet undiscerning. They know facts, quotes, and opinions but struggle to make wise decisions. Wisdom requires filtering information through God's perspective rather than personal preference.

Scripture emphasizes wisdom because wisdom directs life. Knowledge without wisdom creates pride, confusion, and inconsistency. Wisdom without knowledge remains limited. Discernment bridges the two.

God does not ask His people to know everything.
He asks them to discern faithfully.

Discernment Begins Internally

Discernment is not primarily about evaluating others — it begins with examining self.

Unresolved wounds, fear, pride, insecurity, and unhealed trauma distort perception. When the heart is unsettled, discernment weakens. Emotional reactions are mistaken for conviction. Personal bias masquerades as truth.

God refines discernment by refining the inner life. Alignment across the spiritual, mental, emotional, physical, and financial pillars strengthens clarity. When the inner foundation is stable, external confusion loses its power.

Discernment grows where wholeness is cultivated.

Emotion Versus Discernment

Emotion is a powerful signal but a poor compass.

Fear pushes urgency. Anger demands reaction. Excitement creates impulsivity. When decisions are driven primarily by emotion, discernment is bypassed. This does not mean emotion is wrong — it means emotion must be interpreted, not obeyed.

Discernment pauses where emotion wants speed. It asks questions instead of reacting. It allows space for truth to surface.

God's guidance is often quieter than emotional impulse. Discernment trains the heart to listen beneath the noise.

Cultural Pressure and Discernment

Culture rewards conformity. Discernment requires courage.

Living with discernment often means resisting trends, declining popular opinions, and standing firm in convictions that may be misunderstood or criticized. This tension is not new. Scripture consistently shows God's people living counterculturally.

Discernment does not isolate people from culture, but it prevents culture from defining values. God calls His people to influence the world without being absorbed by it.

Alignment requires distinction.

Discernment in Decision-Making

Every decision shapes direction.

Discernment evaluates decisions through alignment rather than convenience. It considers long-term impact, spiritual peace, emotional health, physical capacity, and financial responsibility. It asks whether a choice strengthens wholeness or fragments it.

Discernment often reveals that some opportunities are distractions and some delays are protection. Not every open door is meant to be entered. Not every closed door is failure.

God's discernment protects purpose from unnecessary detours.

Spiritual Discernment and Truth

Spiritual language is easily misused.

Not everything labeled "God's will" reflects God's character. Discernment measures spiritual claims against Scripture, consistency, peace, and fruit. God's truth does not contradict His nature.

Discernment guards against manipulation, spiritual pressure, and false urgency. God does not coerce. He invites.

Where confusion dominates, truth feels grounding.

Discernment Requires Stillness

Noise weakens discernment.

Constant input leaves little room for reflection. Without stillness, the mind cannot process, and the heart cannot settle. Discernment grows in quiet spaces where truth can be weighed rather than rushed.

Stillness is not withdrawal from responsibility. It is preparation for wise engagement.

God often speaks clearly when distractions are reduced.

Discernment in Relationships

Relationships test discernment constantly.

Discernment recognizes when connection is healthy, when boundaries are needed, and when distance is protective. It helps distinguish between compassion and enabling, patience and tolerance, loyalty and self-betrayal.

Godly discernment loves people without losing self. It seeks restoration without ignoring truth.

Healthy relationships require discernment to remain life-giving rather than draining.

Discernment and Accountability

Discernment is strengthened through accountability.

Wise counsel sharpens perception. Trusted voices expose blind spots. Isolation weakens discernment by limiting perspective. God designed community to support clarity, not replace personal responsibility.

Accountability refines discernment rather than threatening it.

Discernment as a Learned Practice

Discernment develops over time.

It grows through obedience, reflection, correction, and experience. Mistakes refine wisdom when humility is present. God does not expect instant discernment — He grows it through faithful practice.

Discernment matures as alignment deepens.

Living Discerned, Not Distracted

A discerning life is not reactive.
It is intentional.

Discernment allows people to move through a confused world without absorbing its confusion. It stabilizes identity, strengthens decision-making, and protects peace. Discernment does not eliminate complexity — it clarifies response.

God designed discernment to keep His people grounded, focused, and aligned regardless of cultural chaos.

Living Aligned Through Discernment

To live **Aligned for Purpose**, discernment must be practiced daily. It is the lens through which truth is recognized, decisions are weighed, and direction is confirmed. Discernment guards the mind, anchors the heart, and preserves alignment in a world that profits from confusion.

God does not leave His people disoriented.
He equips them to see clearly.

Scriptures Referenced in This Chapter

- Proverbs 2:3–6
- Hebrews 5:14
- Romans 12:2
- 1 Corinthians 2:14–16
- James 1:5
- Psalm 119:105

Chapter 28

Discipline That Sustains Freedom

Freedom is not the absence of discipline.
It is the result of it.

One of the greatest misunderstandings in modern life is the belief that discipline restricts freedom. Many people associate discipline with rigidity, punishment, or control, while viewing freedom as spontaneity, ease, and lack of structure. This misunderstanding has caused countless people to abandon the very practices that would protect their peace, clarity, and purpose.

God's design tells a different story.

Discipline does not take freedom away — it **creates** it. It establishes order where chaos would otherwise dominate. It provides stability where emotion would otherwise rule. It protects energy, focus, and integrity so life can be lived intentionally rather than reactively. Without discipline, freedom becomes fragile. With discipline, freedom becomes sustainable.

An aligned life depends on discipline not as a burden, but as a framework that allows purpose to endure.

Why Undisciplined Freedom Collapses

Undisciplined freedom feels liberating at first.

No structure. No limits. No resistance. Decisions are made based on desire, mood, or convenience. Over time, however, this form of freedom begins to erode itself. Energy dissipates. Focus weakens. Boundaries blur. Life becomes reactive rather than directed.

What once felt freeing begins to feel overwhelming.

Without discipline, people become enslaved to impulses — eating patterns, spending habits, emotional reactions, avoidance behaviors, and inconsistent routines. Choice remains, but control diminishes. Discipline is not what removes choice; it is what preserves it.

God's wisdom recognizes that unmanaged desire does not lead to freedom — it leads to bondage.

Discipline as Stewardship, Not Self-Punishment

Discipline is often rejected because it has been taught as self-punishment.

Many people were introduced to discipline through shame-based systems — criticism, harsh correction, or unrealistic expectations. As a result, discipline feels oppressive rather than empowering. God's discipline is different.

Biblical discipline is stewardship.

It is the intentional management of time, energy, body, mind, emotions, and resources. It asks not, "How much can I endure?" but, "What allows me to remain aligned?" Discipline protects what matters most.

God disciplines those He loves not to control them, but to guard their freedom.

Discipline Clarifies Priorities

Life without discipline allows everything to compete equally.

Urgent tasks crowd out important ones. Distractions replace direction. People remain busy yet unfulfilled. Discipline restores order by clarifying priority.

When priorities are disciplined:
time is directed intentionally
energy is preserved
decisions simplify
stress decreases

Discipline does not demand perfection. It demands consistency. Over time, disciplined priorities reduce chaos and increase peace.

God brings order where discipline is practiced faithfully.

Emotional Discipline and Freedom

Emotional discipline is essential to freedom.

Without it, emotions dictate behavior. Anger controls response. Fear determines decisions. Desire overrides wisdom. Emotional discipline does not suppress feelings — it governs them.

Freedom grows when emotions are acknowledged without being obeyed blindly. Discipline allows space between feeling and action. It creates pause, reflection, and choice.

God designed emotional discipline to protect relationships and preserve peace.

Mental Discipline and Clarity

Mental discipline sustains focus.

An undisciplined mind becomes scattered, overwhelmed, and easily influenced. Constant stimulation weakens attention. Without mental discipline, discernment fades and clarity erodes.

Mental discipline includes intentional thought patterns, controlled input, and reflective pauses. It protects the mind from overload and distortion.

Freedom of thought requires discipline of attention.

Physical Discipline and Capacity

The body is not separate from purpose.

Without physical discipline, capacity diminishes. Fatigue increases. Motivation drops. Discipline in rest, movement, nutrition, and recovery protects strength over time.

Physical discipline is not about appearance. It is about sustainability. It allows the body to carry responsibility without breaking down.

God values the body as a vessel for purpose.

Financial Discipline and Peace

Financial freedom does not begin with income.
It begins with discipline.

Without discipline, more money increases anxiety rather than peace. Spending becomes emotional. Saving feels impossible. Debt grows quietly.

Financial discipline creates margin. Margin creates peace. Peace allows generosity without fear.

God's wisdom consistently connects discipline with provision.

Discipline Protects Identity

Discipline reinforces identity.

When identity is rooted in God, discipline becomes an expression of self-respect rather than self-control alone. It says, "I value what God has entrusted to me." Without discipline, identity erodes through compromise and inconsistency.

Discipline aligns behavior with belief.

Consistency strengthens identity more than intention.

Discipline and Delayed Gratification

True freedom requires delayed gratification.

Immediate pleasure often undermines long-term peace. Discipline trains patience — the ability to wait without resentment. This capacity strengthens resilience and maturity.

God often withholds immediate gratification to build endurance and wisdom.

Discipline teaches trust in process rather than impulse.

The Cost of Avoiding Discipline

Avoiding discipline has consequences.

Life becomes reactive. Opportunities are missed. Health deteriorates. Relationships strain. Purpose feels out of reach not because it is unavailable, but because alignment is weak.

Discipline does not eliminate difficulty — it prevents unnecessary struggle.

God invites discipline as protection, not punishment.

Discipline Requires Structure, Not Rigidity

Healthy discipline includes structure without rigidity.

Rigid systems break under pressure. Disciplined systems adapt while preserving values. God's design allows flexibility within alignment.

Discipline should support life, not dominate it.

Structure serves purpose when it remains responsive rather than controlling.

Consistency Over Intensity

Discipline thrives on consistency.

Many people attempt intense change rather than sustainable practice. They push hard briefly, then burn out. God's wisdom favors steady obedience over dramatic effort.

Small disciplines practiced consistently produce lasting freedom.

God values faithfulness over force.

Discipline and Spiritual Alignment

Spiritual discipline anchors life.

Prayer, reflection, Scripture, and stillness are not rituals — they are alignment tools. Without spiritual discipline, faith becomes reactive. With it, faith becomes steady.

God uses spiritual discipline to keep hearts oriented toward truth rather than circumstance.

When Discipline Feels Restrictive

Discipline may feel restrictive initially.

This discomfort is often the resistance of untrained habits rather than the burden of wisdom. Over time, discipline becomes liberating as benefits emerge.

Freedom grows as discipline matures.

God's ways feel narrow only until clarity replaces confusion.

Living a Disciplined, Free Life

A disciplined life is not joyless.
It is intentional.

Discipline allows people to say yes to what matters most without constant exhaustion or regret. It preserves energy, strengthens peace, and protects purpose.

Freedom sustained by discipline lasts.

Discipline as an Act of Trust

Discipline expresses trust in God's design.

It trusts that boundaries bless, that patience pays off, and that obedience produces peace. Discipline says, "I believe alignment matters more than impulse."

God honors disciplined lives because they reflect trust rather than control.

Living Aligned Through Discipline

To live **Aligned for Purpose**, discipline must be embraced as the framework that sustains freedom. It protects identity, preserves peace, and ensures purpose can be lived fully over time.

Discipline does not limit life.
It liberates it.

Scriptures Referenced in This Chapter

- Proverbs 12:1
- Hebrews 12:11
- 1 Corinthians 9:24–27
- Proverbs 25:28
- Galatians 5:22–23
- Luke 16:10

Chapter 29

Purpose Beyond Circumstances

One of the most dangerous misconceptions about purpose is the belief that it is dependent on circumstances.

Many people believe they will live fully once conditions improve — when finances stabilize, relationships heal, health returns, clarity arrives, or opportunity presents itself. Purpose becomes something postponed, waiting for the "right season" to begin. In the meantime, life is endured rather than lived.

God never designed purpose to be seasonal.

Purpose is not suspended by hardship, delayed by uncertainty, or canceled by disruption. It exists independently of circumstance because it is rooted in identity, not environment. When purpose is tied to circumstance, people feel powerless during adversity. When purpose is rooted in God, adversity becomes a context — not a conclusion.

An aligned life understands that purpose is lived *through* circumstances, not after them.

Why Circumstances Feel Like the Gatekeeper of Purpose

Circumstances feel powerful because they affect comfort, control, and predictability.

When circumstances are favorable, people feel confident, motivated, and hopeful. When circumstances deteriorate, confidence weakens, fear rises, and purpose feels distant. This reaction is human, but it is not the design God intends His people to live under.

Circumstances fluctuate constantly. Health changes. Relationships shift. Economies rise and fall. Seasons close unexpectedly. If purpose were dependent on stability, it would be fragile and unreliable.

God anchors purpose in what does not change — His calling, His truth, and His design for your life.

Purpose Is a Way of Living, Not a Destination

Many people treat purpose as a destination to arrive at rather than a way of living daily.

They search for a role, a platform, or a defining moment that will confirm their purpose. Until then, they feel incomplete or misplaced. Scripture presents purpose differently. Purpose is expressed through obedience, faithfulness, integrity, love, and stewardship — regardless of role or recognition.

Purpose is not waiting for you at the end of the journey.
It is revealed through how you walk the journey.

An aligned life does not wait to live purposefully. It chooses purpose in the present.

Living Purposefully in Unfavorable Seasons

Unfavorable seasons often reveal the truest expression of purpose.

When circumstances strip away comfort and control, what remains is character. How a person responds in difficulty reveals what they believe about God, themselves, and life. Purpose lived in hardship looks different, but it is no less real.

Purpose in hardship may look like:
maintaining integrity when compromise feels easier
choosing patience when frustration dominates
serving quietly when recognition disappears
trusting God when outcomes are uncertain

These expressions of purpose are not placeholders. They are essential.

God often does His deepest work through people when circumstances are least cooperative.

The Trap of Waiting for "After"

Waiting for circumstances to improve before engaging purpose creates stagnation.

People tell themselves, "After this season, I'll focus on purpose," not realizing that seasons often overlap and evolve rather than resolve neatly. Waiting trains passivity. It conditions the heart to delay obedience.

God does not ask for purpose later.
He invites purpose now.

Living purposefully now prepares the heart for future opportunity. Delaying purpose weakens readiness.

Purpose When Life Feels Interrupted

Interruptions often feel like derailments.

Plans dissolve. Progress pauses. Momentum breaks. People assume purpose has been interrupted as well. Scripture shows that God frequently uses interruptions as redirections.

Interruptions force reevaluation. They expose misplaced priorities. They refine calling. What feels like disruption may be development.

God's purposes are not fragile.
They are adaptable.

Purpose lived during interruption often becomes more refined and resilient.

Identity as the Anchor of Purpose

Purpose collapses when identity is unstable.

When identity is tied to role, success, or approval, purpose fluctuates with circumstance. When identity is rooted in God, purpose remains steady regardless of external change.

Identity answers *who you are.*
Purpose answers *how you live.*

When identity is secure, purpose flows naturally. Circumstances may alter expression, but not direction.

Purpose in Ordinary Life

Much of life is ordinary.

Routine responsibilities, quiet faithfulness, unseen effort, and repetitive tasks dominate most days. Many people overlook purpose because they expect it to feel extraordinary.

God's design honors ordinary obedience.

Purpose is lived in how you treat people consistently, how you steward what you've been given, and how you remain aligned when no one is watching. Ordinary faithfulness compounds into lasting impact.

God often hides purpose in plain sight.

Purpose Without Visibility

Visibility is not a requirement for purpose.

Many people equate purpose with influence or recognition. When visibility fades, they assume purpose has ended. Scripture consistently contradicts this belief.

Some of the most purposeful lives are lived quietly. God values faithfulness over attention. Visibility may increase or decrease depending on season, but purpose remains.

Purpose without visibility builds humility and depth.

Purpose Through Pain and Loss

Pain does not negate purpose.

Loss, disappointment, and grief can distort perspective, but they do not erase calling. God often redeems pain by transforming it into wisdom, compassion, and discernment that could not have been gained otherwise.

Purpose through pain looks different. It is gentler, deeper, and more grounded. It does not minimize suffering — it allows meaning to emerge through it.

God does not waste pain.
He weaves it into purpose.

Purpose and Responsibility

Purpose is not passive.

It requires responsibility — responsibility to grow, to heal, to steward, to obey. Purpose is not something that happens to you; it is something you live intentionally.

Circumstances may limit options, but they rarely eliminate responsibility. Purpose finds expression through what remains possible.

God measures purpose by faithfulness, not outcomes.

Purpose When You Feel Behind

Feeling behind is common.

Comparison, unmet expectations, and delayed milestones create the illusion of failure. People believe they missed their moment. Scripture reveals that God's timing is personal and precise.

Purpose does not expire.

Feeling behind often signals misaligned expectations rather than missed calling. God's work is not rushed by comparison.

Purpose unfolds in its appointed time.

Purpose Is Strengthened by Faithfulness

Faithfulness fuels purpose.

Each aligned choice reinforces direction. Over time, clarity increases. Confidence stabilizes. Purpose becomes less about uncertainty and more about obedience.

God rarely reveals the full picture at once. Purpose is discovered step by step through faithful living.

Purpose That Cannot Be Taken Away

Circumstances can change roles, locations, and resources. They cannot remove purpose.

Purpose rooted in God cannot be taken by loss, opposition, or delay. It adapts, endures, and matures.

An aligned life understands that purpose is portable.
It goes with you into every season.

Living Purposefully Now

Living purposefully now means choosing alignment today — not waiting for ideal conditions. It means stewarding the present moment faithfully, trusting God to shape the future.

Purpose lived now prepares you for what comes next.

Living Aligned Beyond Circumstances

To live **Aligned for Purpose** means refusing to allow circumstances to define meaning, value, or direction. Purpose remains active in every season, expressed through faithfulness, integrity, and trust.

Your circumstances may change.
Your purpose does not.

Scriptures Referenced in This Chapter

- Romans 8:28
- Ecclesiastes 3:1
- Colossians 3:23–24
- James 1:2–4
- 2 Corinthians 4:16–18
- Psalm 138:8

Chapter 30

Walking in Daily Alignment: Living the Five Pillars as One Life

Alignment is not an idea.
It is a way of living.

Throughout this book, we have explored five essential pillars of God's design for a whole life: **spiritual, mental, emotional, physical, and financial**. Each pillar has been examined individually, not because they exist separately, but because clarity often requires focus. Yet God never designed life to be lived in compartments. He designed it to function as a unified system.

This chapter brings everything together.

Walking in daily alignment means living where all five pillars work together—supporting, correcting, and strengthening one another. When one pillar is neglected, the others strain to compensate. When all five are aligned, life becomes stable, sustainable, and purpose-driven.

This is not about perfection.
It is about **integration**.

The Five Pillars Were Never Meant to Compete

Many people live fragmented lives without realizing it.

They may be spiritually devoted but emotionally unstable.
Mentally sharp but physically depleted.
Financially disciplined but spiritually anxious.
Emotionally compassionate but mentally overwhelmed.

Fragmentation creates internal tension. People feel conflicted without knowing why. They pray but feel restless. They work hard but feel unfulfilled. They believe deeply but live inconsistently.

God's design is not fragmented.

The Five Pillars were created to **support one another**, not operate independently. Spiritual alignment anchors truth. Mental clarity interprets reality. Emotional health regulates response. Physical stewardship sustains capacity. Financial wisdom preserves peace. Together, they form a life that can endure responsibility without collapse.

Spiritual Alignment: The Anchor of the Entire System

The spiritual pillar is the foundation.

Without spiritual alignment, the other pillars lack direction. Spiritual alignment establishes **truth, identity**, and **authority**. It answers the deepest questions of life: *Who am I? Why am I here? Who is guiding me?*

When the spiritual pillar is weak, fear fills the vacuum. People chase control, approval, or security through other means. Mental anxiety increases. Emotional instability follows. Physical burnout becomes common. Financial fear intensifies.

Spiritual alignment does not remove difficulty—it **grounds you within it**.

Daily spiritual alignment looks like:

- Living from identity, not performance
- Obeying truth even when inconvenient
- Trusting God beyond visible outcomes
- Anchoring peace in God rather than circumstance

The spiritual pillar keeps the entire framework oriented toward God rather than self, fear, or culture.

Mental Alignment: Interpreting Life Accurately

The mind is the interpreter of experience.

Mental alignment determines how reality is processed. Without mental clarity, even spiritually grounded people become confused. They misinterpret seasons, internalize false narratives, and struggle with discernment.

Mental alignment filters:

- Thoughts before they become beliefs
- Information before it becomes anxiety
- Emotion before it becomes reaction

A spiritually aligned life without mental discipline becomes vulnerable to distortion. Faith may be sincere, but thinking becomes scattered. Mental alignment brings focus, discernment, and clarity to spiritual truth.

Daily mental alignment includes:

- Guarding what you consume

- Training attention intentionally
- Replacing lies with truth
- Practicing discernment rather than reaction

The mental pillar allows truth to be understood, applied, and lived wisely.

Emotional Alignment: Responding Without Losing Control

Emotions are powerful, but they are not leaders.

Emotional alignment allows feelings to exist without governing behavior. When emotional health is ignored, emotions leak into every area of life—relationships, decisions, work, finances, and faith.

Unaligned emotions distort perception.
Aligned emotions inform response.

Emotionally aligned living looks like:

- Processing pain instead of burying it
- Regulating reactions instead of exploding
- Practicing forgiveness without denial
- Maintaining compassion without self-betrayal

Spiritual truth without emotional health becomes harsh. Mental clarity without emotional awareness becomes detached. Emotional alignment humanizes the entire framework.

God designed emotions to serve wisdom, not replace it.

Physical Alignment: Sustaining the Life God Gave You

The body is not an afterthought.

Physical alignment determines **capacity**. Many people struggle spiritually, mentally, and emotionally because they are physically depleted. Exhaustion amplifies anxiety. Fatigue weakens discipline. Burnout distorts perspective.

Physical alignment is not about appearance.
It is about **sustainability**.

Daily physical alignment includes:

- Honoring rest as obedience
- Managing energy intentionally
- Caring for the body as stewardship
- Respecting limits without guilt

A spiritually passionate life without physical care becomes unsustainable. God never intended purpose to be carried by a broken body.

The physical pillar supports longevity.

Financial Alignment: Removing Fear from Provision

Money touches survival.

When financial alignment is absent, fear dominates decisions. Anxiety replaces trust. People either avoid finances or obsess over them. Both responses disrupt peace.

Financial alignment restores order:

- God as source
- You as steward
- Money as tool

Daily financial alignment includes:

- Discipline without shame
- Generosity without pressure
- Planning without panic
- Contentment without stagnation

Financial alignment does not promise abundance—it promises **peace**. Peace allows purpose to flow without constant fear.

How the Pillars Work Together in Real Life

The Five Pillars constantly interact.

Spiritual truth stabilizes mental clarity.
Mental clarity supports emotional regulation.
Emotional health protects physical energy.
Physical stability strengthens financial discipline.
Financial peace reinforces spiritual trust.

When one pillar weakens, the others compensate—temporarily. Long-term imbalance leads to breakdown. Alignment restores cooperation across the entire system.

This is why healing only one area often fails. God's design requires **whole-life alignment**.

Daily Alignment Is Practiced, Not Achieved

Alignment is not a finish line.

It is a daily practice of recalibration. Some days one pillar requires more attention. Other days another does. Wisdom is knowing where alignment is slipping and responding intentionally rather than reactively.

Daily alignment asks:

- Where am I drifting?

- What needs attention today?
- What truth must I return to?
- What boundary must I honor?

God does not expect constant balance.
He invites consistent **realignment**.

Alignment During Hard Seasons

Alignment matters most when life is difficult.

Hard seasons test integration. Pressure exposes weak pillars. Emotional stress reveals mental habits. Financial strain tests spiritual trust. Physical fatigue challenges discipline.

Aligned living does not prevent hardship.
It prevents collapse within hardship.

When the Five Pillars are practiced together, life remains anchored even when circumstances shift.

The Godly Framework as a Way of Life

This book is not a motivation tool.
It is a **framework for living**.

The Godly Framework is meant to be returned to, revisited, and lived. It is adaptable across seasons, ages, and responsibilities. Whether leading a household, serving a community, building an organization, or rebuilding a life, the Five Pillars remain relevant.

They do not expire.
They mature.

What an Aligned Life Looks Like in Practice

An aligned life:

- Responds rather than reacts
- Discerns rather than follows noise
- Rests without guilt
- Works with purpose
- Handles money without fear
- Leads with humility
- Heals without shame
- Endures without bitterness

This life is not perfect.
It is **grounded**.

Purpose Lived Through Alignment

Purpose is not discovered by chasing it.

Purpose is revealed through alignment.

When the Five Pillars work together, purpose emerges naturally. Decisions clarify. Identity stabilizes. Peace becomes accessible. Impact multiplies.

God designed purpose to flow from wholeness, not striving.

Living the Framework Daily

Living aligned means choosing truth over impulse, wisdom over urgency, and faith over fear—daily. It means honoring the design God established rather than attempting to override it.

The Five Pillars are not restrictions.
They are **protection**.

They guard the life God gave you so it can be lived fully, faithfully, and sustainably.

The Invitation

This chapter is not the end.

It is the beginning of a way of life.

To live **Aligned for Purpose** is to commit to daily alignment across every area of life—spiritual, mental, emotional, physical, and financial—trusting that God's design leads to wholeness.

God does not ask for perfection.
He invites alignment.

And alignment changes everything.

Chapter 31

When All Five Pillars Work Together: The Life God Designed to Function as One

God never designed life to be managed in pieces.

The fragmentation most people experience—burnout, confusion, emotional instability, financial anxiety, spiritual dryness—is not because they lack faith or effort. It is because life is being lived **out of alignment**, with one area overdeveloped while others are neglected. When the Five Pillars are separated, people compensate. When they are integrated, life stabilizes.

This chapter is not about theory.
It is about **function**.

When all five pillars—**spiritual, mental, emotional, physical, and financial**—work together, life begins to operate as God intended. Decisions become clearer. Pressure becomes manageable. Identity stabilizes. Purpose flows without constant strain. Peace becomes accessible even in difficult seasons.

This is not balance as the world defines it.
This is **alignment**.

Why Fragmented Living Fails Over Time

Fragmentation is unsustainable.

A spiritually passionate person who ignores emotional healing eventually becomes reactive or rigid. A mentally sharp person who neglects spiritual grounding becomes anxious or prideful. A physically disciplined person without emotional health becomes controlling. A financially responsible person without spiritual trust becomes fearful. Each pillar, when isolated, eventually turns against the others.

Fragmented living forces constant compensation.

People overwork to avoid emotions.
They overspend to soothe anxiety.
They spiritualize wounds instead of healing them.
They chase discipline without rest.

The result is exhaustion disguised as responsibility.

God's design removes the need for compensation by allowing each pillar to support the others.

The Spiritual Pillar as the Source, Not the Substitute

When all five pillars work together, the spiritual pillar functions correctly—not as a replacement for responsibility, but as the **source of direction**.

Spiritual alignment establishes:

- Identity that is not dependent on performance
- Truth that anchors perception
- Authority that guides decisions
- Peace that is not circumstantial

When spiritual alignment is healthy, it does not bypass mental clarity, emotional processing, physical care, or financial wisdom. Instead, it **informs them**.

Spiritual truth without integration becomes escapism.
Integrated spirituality becomes wisdom.

God's voice clarifies direction, but the other pillars determine how that direction is lived daily.

The Mind as the Interpreter of Spiritual Truth

When the mental pillar is aligned with the spiritual pillar, truth becomes actionable.

The mind interprets what the spirit receives. Without mental clarity, spiritual insight remains abstract. People feel inspired but confused. Convicted but scattered. Motivated but inconsistent.

Mental alignment allows spiritual truth to be:

- Understood accurately
- Applied wisely
- Lived consistently

This is where discernment matures. Thoughts are examined. Lies are challenged. Emotional reactions are filtered. Cultural noise loses influence.

A spiritually grounded but mentally undisciplined life becomes unstable.
A spiritually grounded and mentally aligned life becomes wise.

Emotional Health as the Regulator of Response

When emotional alignment joins spiritual and mental alignment, response becomes regulated instead of reactive.

Emotions no longer hijack decisions. Pain is processed rather than projected. Conflict is handled with wisdom rather than impulse. Compassion is expressed without self-betrayal.

Emotionally aligned living:

- Allows truth without harshness
- Allows boundaries without guilt
- Allows vulnerability without collapse

Emotions become indicators, not dictators.

God designed emotional health to protect relationships, leadership, and endurance. Without it, even strong faith becomes brittle. With it, faith becomes relational and resilient.

The Body as the Carrier of Calling

When physical alignment is added, life gains **capacity**.

The body carries everything else. A depleted body amplifies stress, weakens discipline, and distorts perception. When the physical pillar is aligned, energy stabilizes. Recovery becomes intentional. Limits are honored without shame.

Physically aligned living:

- Supports mental focus
- Stabilizes emotional regulation
- Strengthens spiritual discipline
- Enables financial consistency

God never designed calling to be carried by exhaustion.

A life that honors the body honors longevity.

Financial Alignment as Peace, Not Pressure

When financial alignment integrates with the other four pillars, fear loosens its grip.

Money stops being an emotional regulator. Provision becomes stewardship. Decisions are made with clarity rather than panic. Generosity becomes possible without resentment. Discipline replaces avoidance.

Financial alignment works because:

- Spiritual trust removes fear
- Mental clarity supports planning
- Emotional health prevents impulse
- Physical stability preserves capacity

Money becomes a servant, not a master.

This pillar completes the system by removing survival anxiety that undermines purpose.

How the Pillars Correct One Another

One of the most powerful aspects of the Five Pillars working together is **self-correction**.

When emotional stress rises, mental clarity identifies it.
When physical fatigue increases, emotional regulation responds.
When financial anxiety appears, spiritual truth re-centers trust.
When mental overload grows, physical rest intervenes.

Each pillar checks the others.

This prevents extremes. It protects against burnout, imbalance, and self-deception. God designed this system to be self-stabilizing when practiced intentionally.

What Daily Life Looks Like When All Five Are Aligned

Daily life becomes **responsive instead of reactive**.

You wake with clarity, not dread.
You make decisions with peace, not pressure.
You address conflict without avoidance or aggression.
You work with purpose, not compulsion.
You rest without guilt.
You handle money without fear.

Problems still exist—but they no longer control the system.

Alignment does not remove difficulty.
It removes **disorientation**.

Alignment During Crisis

Crisis exposes integration.

When all five pillars are functioning together, crisis does not collapse the system. It stresses it—but it holds.

Spiritual trust anchors the heart.
Mental clarity prevents panic.
Emotional regulation slows reaction.
Physical care preserves stamina.
Financial discipline prevents desperation.

This is why alignment matters *before* crisis arrives.

God designed wholeness as preparation, not reaction.

Long-Term Transformation Through Integration

Transformation happens over time.

Not through dramatic moments, but through daily alignment. The Five Pillars working together reshape habits, identity, and perspective. Old patterns weaken. New rhythms form. Life becomes less chaotic and more intentional.

This is not self-improvement.
This is **formation**.

God forms people holistically because purpose requires maturity, not intensity.

Why Many Never Experience This Life

Many people touch one or two pillars deeply—but not all five.

They grow spiritually but neglect healing.
They become disciplined but emotionally rigid.
They manage finances but live anxiously.

Partial alignment brings partial results.

God's design requires **integration**.

Wholeness is not optional for sustainability.

The Godly Framework in Motion

This chapter describes the Godly Framework **in motion**, not in theory.

It is a living system—one that adapts across seasons, responsibilities, and callings. Whether rebuilding after loss, leading others, raising a family, serving a community, or carrying a long-term mission, the Five Pillars remain relevant.

They do not compete.
They cooperate.

The Life That Emerges

When all five pillars work together, a distinct kind of life emerges.

A life that is:

- Grounded, not frantic
- Disciplined, not rigid
- Compassionate, not reactive
- Faithful, not fearful
- Purposeful, not pressured

This life reflects God's design—not perfection, but alignment.

Why This Is the Life God Intended

God did not design people to survive life.
He designed them to **live it well**.

The Five Pillars working together restore that design. They create stability where chaos once ruled and peace where fear once dominated.

This is not a shortcut.
It is a framework.

And it works because it reflects the way God designed life to function.

Living This Life Daily

Living this life requires awareness, humility, and consistency.

You will drift.
You will recalibrate.
You will grow.

Alignment is not fragile.
It is resilient.

God meets those who choose alignment daily with grace, clarity, and strength.

The Invitation of Integration

This chapter is not an ending.

It is an invitation to live integrated—spiritually grounded, mentally clear, emotionally healthy, physically sustained, and financially at peace.

This is the life the Five Pillars create **together.**

Chapter 32

The Life That Reflects God's Design: Real-World Traits and Daily Application

A life aligned with God's design is not difficult to recognize.

It does not announce itself loudly. It does not need constant explanation or defense. It is evident in how a person lives, responds, chooses, rests, speaks, works, and relates. Over time, patterns emerge. Stability replaces chaos. Wisdom replaces reaction. Peace becomes visible.

This chapter answers a simple but critical question:

What does a God-designed life actually look like in everyday reality?

Not in sermons.
Not in ideal conditions.
But in traffic, conflict, fatigue, disappointment, responsibility, leadership, money, relationships, pressure, and uncertainty.

When the Five Pillars are fully integrated, the result is not perfection — it is **consistency**. The life that reflects God's design functions coherently. It does not fragment under stress. It adapts without losing identity. It remains grounded regardless of circumstance.

This chapter makes alignment visible.

A God-Designed Life Is Internally Anchored

The most noticeable trait of an aligned life is **internal stability**.

Externally, circumstances may fluctuate. Internally, there is steadiness. Decisions are not rushed. Emotions are not suppressed, but they are not allowed to dominate. Fear does not control direction. Pressure does not dictate values.

This internal anchor comes from spiritual alignment that is supported by mental clarity, emotional regulation, physical sustainability, and financial peace. Because the foundation is internal, external chaos loses authority.

You can see it in how a person pauses before responding.
In how they choose clarity over urgency.
In how they trust without denial.

They are not unbothered — they are **grounded**.

Their Decisions Are Marked by Peace, Not Panic

A God-designed life does not make decisions from panic.

Even when decisions are difficult, there is a noticeable absence of desperation. Choices are made with consideration rather than compulsion. Time is taken to evaluate alignment rather than rush toward relief.

This does not mean indecision.
It means **discernment**.

People living aligned do not chase every opportunity. They do not feel pressured to say yes to everything. They understand that alignment matters more than momentum.

You see this in how they:

- decline without guilt
- wait without anxiety
- choose without second-guessing

Peace becomes a guide — not comfort, not fear, not approval.

They Are Emotionally Present but Not Emotionally Driven

A God-designed life is emotionally honest.

Feelings are acknowledged. Pain is processed. Joy is expressed. Yet emotions do not run the system. There is space between feeling and action.

This person can feel anger without exploding.
Sadness without collapsing.
Joy without losing discipline.

They do not deny emotion — they **regulate** it.

You can see it in how conflict is handled. They listen before responding. They address issues rather than avoid them. They forgive without forgetting wisdom. They love without self-betrayal.

Emotional maturity becomes one of their most visible strengths.

Their Relationships Are Marked by Boundaries and Grace

In a God-designed life, relationships feel safer.

Not because conflict never occurs, but because it is handled honestly. Boundaries are clear. Expectations are realistic. Communication is direct without being harsh.

They do not overextend to gain approval.
They do not manipulate to avoid discomfort.
They do not tolerate what erodes peace.

At the same time, they are gracious. They understand human limitation. They extend forgiveness without enabling harm. They correct without humiliation.

You can see alignment in how they:

- say no without explanation
- say yes with intention
- address problems early
- walk away when necessary

Their relationships are not perfect — they are **healthy**.

They Treat Their Body as a Stewardship, Not a Tool

A God-designed life respects the body.

Not obsessively. Not negligently. But intentionally.

Rest is honored. Limits are acknowledged. Recovery is prioritized. Discipline exists without rigidity. They understand that exhaustion distorts judgment and fatigue amplifies emotion.

They do not glorify burnout.
They do not apologize for rest.

You can see this in how they pace themselves, schedule margin, and protect sustainability. They understand that calling carried by a broken body will eventually collapse.

Physical stewardship becomes an act of obedience rather than vanity.

Their Finances Are Ordered, Not Fear-Driven

In a God-designed life, money is not an emotional regulator.

There is discipline without shame. Generosity without pressure. Planning without panic. Contentment without stagnation.

They know what they have.
They know where it goes.
They know their limits.

You can see it in how they spend intentionally, give wisely, save consistently, and avoid impulsive decisions rooted in emotion.

Money no longer defines worth or direction.
It becomes a **tool**, not a threat.

They Are Consistent Across Environments

One of the clearest indicators of alignment is consistency.

The person you see publicly is the same person privately. Their values do not shift based on audience. Their integrity does not change with convenience.

They do not perform righteousness.
They practice it.

You can see it in how they speak when frustrated, how they behave when tired, and how they handle responsibility when no one is watching.

Consistency replaces image management.

They Respond to Pressure With Wisdom

Pressure does not disappear in a God-designed life — but it does not dominate.

When stress increases, this person slows down rather than speeds up. They assess rather than react. They return to truth rather than impulse.

Crisis reveals integration.

Spiritual trust anchors the heart.
Mental clarity prevents panic.
Emotional regulation slows reaction.
Physical discipline preserves stamina.
Financial wisdom prevents desperation.

You can watch them remain composed when others unravel — not because they are superior, but because they are aligned.

They Live With Purpose Without Obsession

Purpose in a God-designed life is lived, not chased.

They do not strive to prove worth through productivity. They do not attach identity to outcomes. They serve faithfully without needing constant validation.

Purpose becomes a **posture**, not a performance.

You can see it in how they show up consistently, steward what is in front of them, and trust God with outcomes.

They are present.
They are faithful.
They are steady.

They Accept Correction Without Defensiveness

A God-designed life remains teachable.

Correction is not viewed as rejection. Feedback is not perceived as threat. Growth is welcomed without shame.

This person can admit mistakes, adjust course, and recalibrate without collapsing identity.

Humility becomes visible strength.

They Recalibrate Regularly, Not Perfectly

Alignment is maintained through recalibration.

They notice drift early. They respond intentionally. They do not wait for crisis to make adjustments. They reflect, realign, and continue forward.

Failure becomes information, not identity.

This is how longevity is preserved.

Their Life Creates Peace for Others

Perhaps the most tangible trait of a God-designed life is this:

People feel safer around them.

Not controlled.
Not impressed.
Not intimidated.

But calmer. Clearer. More grounded.

Their presence reduces chaos rather than amplifying it. Their words bring perspective rather than pressure. Their leadership stabilizes rather than dominates.

Peace becomes contagious.

What This Life Is Not

A God-designed life is not:

- perfect
- problem-free
- emotionless
- passive
- religious performance

It is **integrated**.

The Invitation to Live This Way

This chapter does not describe a rare personality type.

It describes a **practice**.

Anyone willing to live aligned across the Five Pillars can live this way — gradually, imperfectly, faithfully.

The Godly Framework is not a theory to admire.
It is a way of life to inhabit.

The Life God Designed Is Livable

God did not design life to be survived.
He designed it to be lived with clarity, peace, endurance, and purpose.

This is the life the Five Pillars create together.

Not someday.
Not later.

Daily.

Final Conclusion — Choosing Alignment as a Way of Life

Every life eventually answers the same question, whether intentionally or unconsciously:
Will I live by design, or will I live by default?

Most people never consciously choose default living. It happens quietly. Life speeds up. Responsibilities stack. Pressure increases. Survival replaces intention. Over time, days are lived reacting instead of deciding, coping instead of building, enduring instead of aligning. Nothing dramatic breaks—yet something essential erodes.

This book was written to interrupt that erosion.

Not by offering another motivational push, another spiritual checklist, or another set of ideas to admire—but by restoring awareness of how life was meant to function. Alignment is not about doing more. It is about living rightly ordered. It is about choosing coherence over chaos, truth over noise, and intentionality over drift.

The greatest danger is not failure.
It is misalignment sustained long enough to feel normal.

Alignment Is a Decision, Not a Personality Trait

One of the most liberating truths is this: alignment is not reserved for a certain type of person.

It is not dependent on temperament, background, education, or circumstances. It is not reserved for leaders, mystics, entrepreneurs, or the unusually disciplined. Alignment is a decision—made repeatedly—to live in agreement with truth rather than convenience.

You do not drift into alignment.
You choose it.

And that choice is available in every season of life—whether rebuilding, leading, waiting, grieving, growing, or simply maintaining. Alignment does not require ideal conditions. It requires awareness and willingness.

The Cost of Alignment Is Real—and Worth It

Alignment is not free.

It costs comfort when comfort conflicts with truth.
It costs speed when speed replaces wisdom.
It costs approval when approval requires compromise.

Alignment often requires slowing down in a world that rewards urgency. It requires saying no where others say yes. It requires honoring limits where culture glorifies excess. It requires integrity where shortcuts are normalized.

But the cost of misalignment is always greater.

Misalignment costs peace.
It costs clarity.
It costs health, relationships, and longevity.

Alignment may feel demanding at first, but misalignment is exhausting over time.

This Is Not About Control—It Is About Order

Alignment is often misunderstood as control.

In reality, alignment releases control by restoring order. Control is driven by fear. Alignment is driven by trust. Control attempts to force outcomes. Alignment submits to truth and responds wisely.

When life is aligned, fewer decisions are made from panic. Fewer reactions are driven by emotion. Fewer sacrifices are made unnecessarily. Life becomes simpler—not easier, but clearer.

Order creates freedom.
Disorder creates pressure.

Alignment Does Not Eliminate Difficulty—It Changes How Difficulty Is Carried

This framework does not promise a life without hardship.

Challenges will still come. Loss will still occur. Uncertainty will still arise. What changes is not the presence of difficulty, but the way it is handled.

Aligned lives bend without breaking.
They adapt without losing identity.
They endure without becoming bitter.

Alignment does not remove weight—it distributes it correctly so collapse is no longer inevitable.

You Will Drift—Recalibration Is the Practice

No one remains perfectly aligned forever.

Drift is human. Fatigue, distraction, pressure, and transition pull life out of order. Alignment is not maintained by perfection, but by **recalibration**.

The aligned life is not the one that never drifts—it is the one that notices drift early and responds intentionally.

Recalibration is wisdom, not failure.

The Measure of This Life Is Not Applause

A life lived by God's design will not always be celebrated.

It may be misunderstood.
It may appear slower.
It may look less impressive on the surface.

But over time, it reveals something rare: **stability**.

And stability becomes influence.

People trust what lasts.
They follow what remains steady.
They are drawn to what feels safe, grounded, and real.

Alignment produces a life that quietly leads without demanding attention.

This Framework Is Not Finished—It Is Lived

This book does not end with a command to do something new.

It ends with an invitation to live differently.

Not dramatically.
Not performatively.
But consistently.

Alignment is practiced in ordinary decisions, repeated behaviors, honest self-awareness, and daily responsibility. It is lived in kitchens, workplaces, conversations, budgets, schedules, rest, conflict, and recovery.

The most powerful lives are not built in moments of intensity—but in patterns of faithfulness.

The Choice That Remains

Now that you see the design, the choice is yours.

You can admire it without adopting it.
You can agree with it without living it.
Or you can choose alignment—imperfectly, steadily, intentionally.

God does not demand mastery.
He invites agreement.

Agreement with truth.
Agreement with order.
Agreement with a life that functions as it was designed to function.

Alignment changes everything—not overnight, but over time.

And over time, that is what matters most.

Final Word

You were not designed to survive life.
You were designed to live it whole.

That life is possible.
That life is sustainable.
That life begins with alignment.

And alignment begins with a choice—today, not someday.

Choose alignment.

---

www.ingramcontent.com/pod-product-compliance
Lightning Source LLC
Chambersburg PA
CBHW071815230426
43670CB00013B/2465